January 6: Was This Nancy Pelosi's Illegal Entrapment Scheme? What Would a Jury Find?

Nigel Nobbs

ISBN: 9798390145227
ISBN-13:

This book is dedicated to Emily, our wild, reckless, high spirited, energetic, curious, loving, caring daughter who was murdered by a shot in her head on June 4, 2013 at age 22. We never found out what happened and never will until we see her in heaven. There were no witnesses. Our hearts are broken and always will be. As Reverend Crews said, "Emily was like a shooting star, rocketing through the night sky, lighting up the lives of everyone she met."

June 20, 1991 - June 4, 2013. RIP Emily. We love you.

TABLE OF CONTENTS

* * *

INTRODUCTION: PELOSI'S ROLE IN PLANNING THE JANUARY 6 VIOLENCE

Did Nancy Pelosi plan the breach of the Capitol Building on January 6, 2021 along with the associated violence? Would a jury or a judge likely find her guilty in a criminal case or liable in a civil case for her actions or inactions leading up to and including January 6? This book presents the evidence and arguments as to whether or not it is likely that a jury or a judge would find that Pelosi planned the breach of the building and the violence, and whether or not she would likely be found guilty of various crimes, and liable for money damages.

What motives might Pelosi have had to plan the breach and violence? She had two, at least. Who would have benefited for the breach of the Capitol Building, causing the end of the Republican challenge to the certification of the election? Nancy Pelosi, not Trump. She knew that if the building were breached, that would end the Republican's challenge to the certification, and Congress would simply certify the election the next day after the rioters had been removed. On January 6, before the breach, the Republicans were asking that the certification of the election be delayed for one week so that an audit of the voting could be done. The Democrats were seeking to have the vote certified on January 6, despite evidence of voter fraud and irregularities. Pelosi would not have cared if the certification of the vote was delayed because Congress could simply hold the certification at a later date. But she benefited greatly by the breach because the Republican strategy of challenging the certification would in fact be permanently stopped by a breach. Trump was the one who was damaged the most by a breach. His followers knew that. That is, his real followers. The Trump haters embedded in the crowd also knew that.

Pelosi's second motive was her desire to damage Trump in any way she could, and as viscously as she could. She hated and still hates

President Donald J. Trump. A breach of the Capitol Building by so called Trump 'supporters', even if they were undercover FBI informants, would do immense damage to the former president, and if Pelosi's plan worked, might lead to criminal charges.

Democrats have attempted to block the certification of various elections on numerous occasions. So it's ironic that the Liberals considered the Republicans' attempt to block the certification in 2021 to be an attack on our democracy. For example, Rep. Jamie Raskin (D-Md) and others objected to Trump's certification in 2016, and can be seen on video doing that. Raskin, that fool, was the lead impeachment manager in one of Trump's impeachments. How did that go for you Jamie? Raskin also sat on the so called January 6 committee, which allowed hearsay evidence (Hutchinson), didn't allow cross-examination, didn't allow the other side to present evidence, would publish partial but not all of a witness's testimony to the public, would hide evidence, would fabricate false evidence, hid exculpatory evidence and purposely did not investigate evidence that harmed their side (Pelosi's emails refusing security). But Liz Cheney is a 'firm believer in the rule of law.' She's a joke.

There is plenty of evidence to support the conclusion that Pelosi planned and enabled the breach of the Capitol Building. The most damning piece of evidence is that she declined Trump's several requests a few days prior to January 6 to bring in the National Guard to protect the building. She also failed to properly deploy and reinforce the Capitol Police. They report to her. She had received, prior to January 6, several intelligence reports stating that there was likely going to be violence and an attack on the building. She wanted the building to be breached.

Another strong piece of evidence implicating Pelosi in the violence on January 6 is that the upper tier of the FBI is strongly tied to and aligned with the Democratic party, and the FBI, not Trump supporters, were the ones who attacked police, and broke into the Capitol Building. Trump supporters defended themselves from police violence that was provoked by FBI informants, and his supporters entered the building only after FBI informants opened doors and broke windows into the building. The police waived Trump people into the building, and politely escorted them around the inside of the building, for the most part, with a few brutal exceptions. Pelosi is one of two or three defacto heads of the Democrat Party, and so has back channel connections into the Democrat aligned upper tier of the FBI.

Other evidence against Pelosi includes:

- Pelosi prohibited the January 6 Committee from subpoenaing, demanding or looking at her emails, texts and correspondence relating to January 6.

- Pelosi has refused to release 14,000 hours of security video taken by the security system at the Capitol Building, showing FBI informants opening the building's doors from the inside, and encouraging protesters to commit violent acts. The video also shows the police inviting people into the building, shows most protesters doing nothing more than walking around and taking photos, and shows police violently beating innocent protesters.

- Pelosi knew ahead of time that FBI informants dressed as Trump supporters would break into the Capitol Building, and so she had a film crew stationed inside the building to film the violence.

- Trump had had over 100 rallies prior to January 6, and there never had been any violence. Did this change of January 6 because of FBI informants?

The evidence against Pelosi will be discussed in more detail in later chapters.

* * *

"Former Clinton White House and feminist author Naomi Wolf has issued a "formal letter of apology" to Republicans and conservatives after believing what she describes as "lies" about Jan. 6, 2021. … Wolf … wrote that "the peaceful Republicans and conservatives as a whole have been demonized by the story told by Democrats in leadership of what happened that day" after new footage of the Capitol breach was aired by Fox News host Tucker Carlson last week.

"'Republicans, conservatives, I am sorry. I also believed wholesale so much else that has since turned out not to be as I was told it was by NPR, MSNBC and the New York Times,' Wolf wrote on Substack. 'Anyone in leadership who misrepresented to the public the events of the day so as to distort the complexity of its actual history — must be held accountable.'"[1]

Of course anyone who threatened or attacked police officers, or caused property damage should be prosecuted under our normal standards of justice, including all FBI agents and informants who threatened, encouraged, attacked or destroyed property. Protesters should not be thrown in jail for 2 years waiting for trials.

Of course anyone who threatened or attacked police officers, or caused property damage should be prosecuted under our normal standards of justice, including all FBI agents and informants who threatened, encouraged, attacked or destroyed. Protesters should not be persecuted like Putin's political prisoners, as Attorney General Garland has done, and held in pre-trial detention for 2 years, some in solitary confinement without medical treatment. They should be released on bail pending their trials as is common in our judicial

---

[1] "Former Clinton White House Adviser Issues an Apology to Conservatives," *The Epoch Times*, March 15 - 21, 2023, A2.

system. Prosecutors should provide all exculpatory evidence as required under our constitution. Prosecutors have failed to do so, and they should be fired, permanently lose their law licenses and pensions, and be liable for civil damages, without any government indemnification, since their actions were reckless. This punishment should also be doled out to Merrick Garland who has authorized this bizarre persecution. No one who was waived or tacitly invited into the building by the police should be arrested or prosecuted for any reason. But yes, protesters who broke the law should be fairly prosecuted.

STANDARDS OF PROOF IN CIVIL AND CRIMINAL CASES

Before a defendant is found guilty in a criminal case, the prosecutor must provide enough proof to convince the jury that he truly did commit the crime. Likewise, a defendant cannot be ordered to pay a plaintiff in a civil case unless the plaintiff's attorney has provided adequate proof of the defendant's liability. But, how much proof is enough? Here are the legal standards of proof for civil and criminal cases:

Preponderance of the Evidence

Preponderance of the evidence is the legal standard of proof that is used in the majority of civil lawsuits, including personal injury cases. To meet this legal standard of proof, the plaintiff in a civil case must provide evidence that shows there is a greater than 50% chance that the defendant is liable. To put it simply, the plaintiff must show that the defendant is more likely than not liable for the damages.

For example, let's say a jury is deciding whether a defendant is liable for the car accident that caused the plaintiff's injuries. The jury decides that 60% of the evidence shows that the defendant is liable, but the other 40% of the evidence does not or is questionable. In this situation, the jury must rule in favor of the plaintiff because she was able to provide a preponderance of evidence showing the defendant's liability.

Beyond A Reasonable Doubt

The beyond a reasonable doubt legal standard of proof is used solely in criminal cases. This is the highest legal standard of proof, meaning more evidence is required to prove this legal standard of proof than any other.

Contrary to popular belief, "beyond a reasonable doubt" does not mean that the jury must be 100% convinced of the defendant's guilt in order to reach a guilty verdict. It simply means that the jury must find a defendant guilty if the evidence is so convincing that it would be impossible for a reasonable person to doubt the defendant's guilt. The jury must ask themselves if there is any other logical conclusion that can be reached based on the evidence. If there could be another logical explanation for the evidence besides that the defendant committed the crime, the prosecutor has not met this legal standard of proof.

CIRCUMSTANTIAL EVIDENCE V DIRECT EVIDENCE

"Evidence typically falls into two broad categories. Direct evidence is evidence that can prove something all by itself. In California, jurors are given the example of a witness who saw that is was raining outside the courthouse. Jurors are instructed, "If a witness testifies he saw if raining outside before he came into the courthouse, that testimony is direct evidence that it was raining."[2] This testimony (if it is trustworthy) is enough, in and of itself, to prove that it is raining. On the other hand, circumstantial evidence (also known as *indirect evidence*) does not prove something on its own, but points us in the right direction by proving something related to the question at hand. This related piece of evidence can then be considered (along with additional pieces of circumstantial evidence) to figure out what happened. Jurors in California are instructed, "For example, if a witness testifies that he saw someone come inside wearing a raincoat covered with drops of water, that testimony is circumstantial evidence because it may support a conclusion that it was raining outside.[3]" The more pieces of consistent circumstantial evidence, the more reasonable the conclusion. If we observed a number of people step out of the courthouse for a second, then duck back inside, soaked with little spots of water on their clothing, or saw more people coming into the courthouse, carrying umbrellas, and dripping with water, we would have several additional pieces of evidence that could be used to make the case that it was raining. The more cumulative the circumstantial evidence, the better the conclusion."

Even without any direct evidence but with only circumstantial evidence, a lawyer can prove the truth of a factual issue beyond a

---

[2] Judicial Council of California, *Judicial Council of California Criminal Jury Instructions*, CalCrim Section 223.

[3] Ibid, Section 223.

reasonable doubt.[4]

"Jurors are instructed to make no qualitative distinction between direct and circumstantial evidence in a case. Judges tell jurors, "Both direct and circumstantial evidence are acceptable types of evidence to prove or disprove the elements of a charge, including intent and mental state and acts necessary to a conviction, and neither is necessarily more reliable than the other. Neither is entitled to any greater weight than the other.[5]" Juries make decisions about the guilt of suspects in cases that are completely circumstantial every day. ... [Almost all cold-case homicides] have been successfully prosecuted with nothing but circumstantial evidence.[6]"

Circumstantial evidence can be more reliable than direct evidence. Eye witness testimony is direct evidence, but some studies have shown that over time, some eye witnesses have trouble correctly identifying a person from a line-up, even though they had clearly seen the person at the time of the crime. Memory can become fuzzy over time.

*   *   *

The following hypothetical murder demonstrates how direct versus circumstantial evidence is used to try to prove the facts in a case. In a quiet residential neighborhood on a sunny day someone screams from one of the houses. A witness is in her yard, hears the

---

[4] Ibid, 57.

[5] Judicial Council, Section 223.

[6] Wallace, 57.

screams and sees through a window or her neighbor's house a man assaulting her neighbor in the living room. She then saw the man run out the front door holding a bloody baseball bat. She got a long look at his face as he ran to a car and drove off.

* * *

When the witness is in the witness stand in court testifying that the defendant is the man she saw killing the victim, she would be providing *direct evidence*. This one piece of direct evidence would be enough to prove the defendant committed the murder, assuming you could trust what the witness had to say.

Now suppose the facts are different, and the suspect had been wearing a mask, and so the witness could not identify the suspect, other than his general build and clothing. With this information alone, it is impossible to prove that any particular suspect was the true killer. There is no direct evidence in the case.

The detectives develop a potential suspect from the victim's social contacts, Joe, and they begin to collect evidence, circumstantial not direct evidence.

- Joe fits the general physical description.

- Joe first hesitated to provide an alibi. Then when he did, upon investigation, it turned out to be a lie.

- Most people would not be willing to convict Joe based on this evidence.

- Joe admitted recently breaking up with the victim after a rocky romantic relationship. He admitted to recently arguing with her about the relationship, and was extremely nervous when the detectives focused on her. He repeatedly tried to minimize his relationship with her.

- Is Joe guilty? There might be other reasonable explanations to what we've seen so far. There isn't enough evidence to be certain of his guilt.

- The detectives learn that Joe had entered the victim's house and appeared to be waiting for her when she returned home. There was no signed of forced entry, and Joe was one of only two people who had keys to the house.

- The circumstantial evidence is growing with every revelation. Joe seems to be "a person of interest."

- A friend of Joe's approaches the detectives and tells them that he found a suicide note at Joe's house that was dated on the day of the murder, and describes Joe's deparate state of ming and his desire to kill himself on the afternoon that followed the killing.

- Given all the suspicious evidence, a judge signs a search warrant for Joe's house.

- The detectives discover a hidden baseball bat, that is dented in a way that is inconsistent with its use in baseball. The crime lab found there was no blood on the bat, but it had recently been cleaned with bleach. They also found a pair of jeans that had been chemically spot cleaned in two areas in the front of the legs. No blood was found on the jeans.

- The detectives also found a pair of boots with a unique stripe up the side. The witness had said that the suspect had worn boots with a unique stripe up the side. The detectives talked to local vendors who said that this brand of boots was unusual for the area. Only two stores sold the boots, and ten pairs had been sold in the past five years. Joe owned one of those ten pairs.

- Many people would now conclude that Joe was the guilty given the above circumstantial evidence.

- ◦ The witness said that the suspect ran into a black, older Karnann Ghia car. The detectives found a black, older Karnann Ghia parked in Joe's garage.

- ◦ Given all that we know, the only reasonable explanation is that Joe is the killer. It is *possible* that Joe is just unlucky enough to suffer from an unfortunate alignment of coincidences that make him appear to be guilty when he is not. But it is not reasonable to think he is just unlucky. Everything points to Joe, and his guilt is the only reasonable conclusion when all the circumstantial evidence is considered cumulatively. A jury must look at the evidence as a whole, and not as individual pieces of evidence. A jury is asked to return a verdict that is based on what is reasonable, not possible.

- ◦ The case against Joe id *entirely* circumstantial. This is not a single piece of forensic or eyewitness evidence that directly links him to the crime.

*   *   *

A jury just (March 2023) found Alex Murdaugh guilty of murdering his wife and son in South Carolina using only circumstantial evidence, and zero direct evidence. He was sentenced to 30 years in prison.

In March 2023, a South Florida man was released from custody Monday after serving 34 years in prison for a crime he didn't commit. The man was convicted based on direct evidence, eyewitness testimony. This evidence turned out to be false. "Sidney Holmes dreamed of this moment for decades. "I knew this day was going to come, sooner or later," Holmes said. "Today is the day. When he walked out of custody, family members embraced him one by one.

His mother, Mary Holmes, cried tears of joy."I'm just so grateful to God," she said. "I'm just so grateful to everybody that made this possible."

"I'm excited to see my big cousin come home and just happy for him to be here," cousin Kevin Hill said. "I can't wait for the second half of life to start."

Holmes was arrested in 1988 and convicted the following year of being the getaway driver for two men who robbed a man and woman at gunpoint outside a store and stole their car near Fort Lauderdale.

Holmes, now 57, was sentenced to 400 years in state prison.Officials said he contacted the state attorney's conviction review unit in 2020.

After investigating, they found that there was no evidence linking Holmes to the robbery and that *eyewitnesses* (that is, direct evidence) *likely confused him with someone else.*

"We had the opportunity to exonerate a man who's been in prison wrongfully," Broward County State Attorney Harold Pryor said. "We had the opportunity to do the right thing today, to right a wrong."

Once he learned he was finally free, Holmes broke down in tears while in court Monday, embracing Pryor.[7]"

Obviously, in this case, direct evidence resulted in destroying a man's life. Did the prosecutors know that their eyewitness direct evidence was faulty, but they didn't care because they needed to convict someone, anyone, to protect their jobs, or for career advancement? Prosecutors do such things. Look at the horrible January 6 prosecutors. Or did they not care because Holmes is Black?

---

[7] Kim Wynne, "Broward County Man exonerated for a crime he didn't commit," WPTV.com, March 15, 2023.

*   *   *

* * *

In the majority of cases scientific conclusions are based solely on circumstantial evidence, and not on direct evidence. Most people consider science to be a definitive, 'hard' field, where conclusions can generally be considered 'true,' and an accurate description of the world around us. So since science itself is often based on purely circumstantial evidence, then a 'soft' field like the law should also be allowed to be based only on circumstantial evidence.

For example, "The theory of plate tectonics , which revealed the earth's crust to be a set of interlocking plates that are always forming, disintegrating, and gringing together locked wrestlers locked in a clinch, wouldn't be proposed until 1912 — thirty years after Darwin's death …. Even so, it was regarded as a fringe theory for decades and wasn't widely accepted until a new generation of geologists tested and confirmed it in the 1960's"[8] No scientist has ever direct evidence of the earth's plates moving, but the circumstantial evidence is overwhelming. They have seen fault lines, but those aren't plates moving, but they are strong circumstantial evidence.

When mammals hair in the course of evolution is important for those who study paleoevolution. Hair is crucial for the survival of most mammals. The evidence for hair is all circumstantial. "Regardless, there is a stronger line of evidence for hair; many therapsid fossils are pocked with pits and grooves of their facial bones, similar to the canals that bring blood and nerves to the whiskers of mammals today." Circumstantial evidence.

---

[8] Jonathan Meiburg, *A Most Remarkable Creature, The Hidden Life and Epic Journey of the World's Smartest Bird of Prey* (New York, Alfred A. Knopf, 2021), 117.

President Garfield would not have died from the bullet lodged in his body if the prevalent view of the experts had not been followed, and had the circumstantial evidence been followed. This evidence, from by Mr. Lister, was that infections were caused by bacteria on dirty medical tools. Garfield died from infections, not from the bullet. The experts ignored Lister's evidence and stuck all sorts of filthy things into the bullet hole. Garfield died while trying to recuperate on the Jersey Shore.

The 18,000 people who died from malaria during the building of the Panama Canal could have been saved had the 'experts' not ignored the circumstantial evidence. This evidence was that a parasite in a certain species of mosquito caused malaria. This 'experts' said it was caused by vapors coming out of the ground from the steam shovels building the canal. The doctors even put the legs of the patients' bed in bowls of water to prevent ants from climbing onto the beds. The malaria mosquitoes breeded in the bowls. The doctors housed non-malaria patients with malaria patients. The mosquitoes spread malaria to the non-malaria patients.

Quantum physics is cutting edge physics, widely accepted, and based almost completely on circumstantial evidence. It is the study of subatomic particles such as electrons and particles smaller than electrons. It's conclusions are bizarre. The same particle can exist in two different places at the same time. A particle can have a sister particle and the two are a million miles away from each other. If a change is made to one, then the same change appears simultaneously in the other, faster than the speed of light, and known as quantum entanglement. Quantum physics is used in making super computers. If physicists can spend hundreds of millions of dollars making super computers based on circumstantial evidence, then jurors can use circumstantial evidence to determine Pelosi's guilt or innocence, or civil liability for huge amounts of monetary damages.

PELOSI'S SABOTAGED THE SECURITY AT THE CAPITOL

The most damning piece of evidence that Pelosi planned and enabled the breach of the Capitol Building is that she took multiple steps to sabotage the security at the building. She *wanted* the building to be breached. A breach benefited her. A breach benefited the Democrats.

Pelosi's sabotage of building security took two forms. First, she blocked her staff, underlings and others from providing adequate security. Second, she instructed the Capitol Police, through her underlings, to invite, entice and push Trump supporters into the building, thereby framing the supporters, and then Garland at the DOJ arrested them for trespass and other false charges. The Capitol Police under Pelosi tricked Trump supporters to go into the building by removing outside metal barriers when protesters arrived, and by waiving and inviting the protesters into the building.

* * *

Pelosi Actively Blocked Security

She declined Trump's several requests a few days prior to January 6 to bring in the National Guard to protect the building. She also failed to properly deploy and reinforce the Capitol Police. She controlled the Capitol police since she was the Speaker of the House. She had received, prior to January 6, many intelligence reports stating that there was likely going to be violence and an attack on the building.

Who was in charge of security in addition to Pelosi? Security was shared by the Capitol Police, the FBI and the DC Police. Prior to January 6 the Department of Defense contacted the Capitol Police, the Sergeant at Arms for the House and the Sergeant at Arms for the Senate, and recommended that the National Guard be deployed prior to January 6, and also the DOD requested that Capitol Police, and the two sergeant at arms authorize that the guard be deployed. The police and sergeant of arms declined the requests.

A Supreme Court decision states that two things must happen to deploy the National Guard. First, the president must authorize the use of the National Guard. He does not have the power to order the guard. Second, then the governor, mayor of DC or federal law enforcement, as the case may be, must request that the guard be deployed.

Trump did authorize the guard as reported by Trump's acting chief of staff, Cash Patel. On January 4 Pelosi had rejected the deployment of the Nation Guard.[9] The Department of Defense told the Mayor of DC, Muriel Bowser, and the Capitol Police that Trump had authorized the deployment of 20,000 troops. Both the mayor and the police declined the troops, in letters, which are available to the public. The DOD request is also in writing, and available to the public. So when a liberal claims that Trump did not authorize the troops, the liberal is lying, as is the nature of liberals.

Trump had no power or authority to secure the Capitol. It was not his job to do so. That job was the sergeant at arms of Congress and the sergeant at arms for the Senate, and they reported to Pelosi and Schumer, and that RINO, Chinese controlled old fool Mitch McConnell.

---

[9] Julie Kelly, *January 6: How the Democrats Used The Capitol Protest To Launch A War of Terror On the Political Right* (New York: Post Hill Press, 2022)

The head of the Capitol Police on January 6, Steven Sund, testified to the January 6 Committee that on January 4 and 5 he asked numerous times for more security, and was denied by Democrats, Republicans and the Capitol Police Board. There were National Guardsmen at the DC Armory on January 6, but they were not deployed until after the protest had ended, at 5:40 in the afternoon. The Guard would have prevented the breach of the building. The January 6 Committee did not look into why Pelosi failed to deploy the Guard that day.

The Capitol Police recklessly and illegally threw flash bangs into a group of Trump supporters who were legally standing outside the building and who were threatening no one and causing no damage. The police did not want the Guard present as the Guard would have stopped the police from throwing the flash bombs.

Former Capitol Police lieutenant Tarik K. Johnson told The Epoch Times and Tucker Carlson (Tucker Carlson show March 7, 2023) that he "begged for help all day long on Jan. 6 2021, and I feel I was largely ignored. … There was no response from anybody at the Command Center. … I heard no response. Then I asked for permission to evacuate. I heard no response." Johnson said that a top Capitol Police commander, Yogananda Pittman, failed to response to urgent radio calls to evacuate the US Congress. Senator Ron Johnson (R-Wis) said, "that many people responsible for security that day have repeatedly failed to cooperate with the Congressional investigation."

Why have they failed to cooperate?

The Associated Press reported that Bowser had called up 340 National Guard troops to help with traffic and crowd control. D.C.

Metropolitan Police, according to the agency's chief, "was fully deployed on 12-hour shifts the week of January 4, with days off and leave canceled." But Bowser also sent a letter on January 5 to the acting Attorney General, acting Secretary of Defense, and Secretary of the Army confirming that "the District of Columbia is not requesting other federal law enforcement personnel and discourages any additional deployment without immediate notification to, and consultation with [D.C] MPD if such plans are underway."

Pelosi has said she was not involved with security. Representative Marjorie Taylor Greene claims that is a lie. To back up her claims, Greene cited a scathing report from House Republicans that contain emails and text messages, exposing the truth that Pelosi was involved in security measures for that day.

"Then-House Sergeant at Arms Paul Irving — who served on the Capitol Police Board by virtue of his position — succumbed to political pressures from the Office of Speaker Pelosi and House Democrat leadership leading up to January 6, 2021," the report read, adding "he coordinated closely with the Speaker and her staff and left Republicans out of important discussions related to security."

Irving reportedly "coordinated closely" with Pelosi and her staff on security plans for Jan. 6, however, Republicans were purposely left out of "important discussions related to security."

Irving argued that Pelosi and House Democrats were "compromised by politics and did not adequately prepare for violence at the Capitol."

The report, which was released by Jim Banks (R-IN), Jim Jordan (R-OH), Rodney Davis (R-IL), Kelly Armstrong (R-ND), and Troy Nehls (R-TX), said that "the Speaker's office was heavily involved in planning and decision-making before and during the events of Jan. 6, 2021, and micromanaged the Sergeant at Arms."

Despite Pelosi continually saying she "has no power over the

Capitol Police," the outgoing House Speaker spoke to Irving 36 times about Capitol security and attended meetings in December 2020 leading up to the protests.[10]

*   *   *

The January 6 Committee Hid its Findings of Security Failures

Pelosi instructed the January 6 Committee to suppress the committee's finding that there were multiple security failures by the Capitol Police and others that materially contributed to the breach of the building. Pelosi created the January 6 Committee, it was run by Democrats, and the only two Republicans on the committee were deranged, psychopathic Trump haters. Pelosi refused to seat the two members that the Republican leadership, Kevin McCarthy, appointed.

On February 2, NBC News interviewed Tim Heaphy, the lead investigator for the committee. He stated that the January 6 Committee always had a large amount of information about the security failures on January 6, and that Pelosi failed to act on the information. He stated that the intelligence was very specific and the Feds could have prevented the January 6 conflict. People familiar with the committee said that the committee downplayed the information about the security failures because the committee wanted to focus on Trump.[11]

Heaphy stated that the FBI and the Department of Homeland Security failed to act on the intelligence. The committee hid this information. Instead of providing security, the FBI put informants into the crowd.

Former Capitol Hill Police Chief Steven Sund stated that Pelosi and her staff were warned about the intelligence on potential bad actors within the protesters, but Pelosi's sergeant at arms, Paul Irving, did not want the National Guard because that would give 'bad optics.' He denied the request for the guard. Sund also spoke to the

---

[10] Sarah Arnold, "Scathing Report Reveals Nancy Pelosi Was Responsible For Failed Jan. 6 Security Measures," *TownHall*, Dec 22, 2022.

[11] Tucker Carlson Show, Fox News, Feb.3, 2023.

Senate sergeant at arms Mike Stenger on January 4, and Sund said Stenger told him that "Speaker Pelosi will never go for the National Guard.[12]"

So why would Pelosi block necessary security forces, and why did she later instruct the committee to hide the fact that they had concluded that the poor security had been a major cause of the Capitol violence?

*   *   *

Pelosi Had the Police Waive People Into the Capitol Building

There are over 50 videos taken with cell phones at the Capitol Building on January 6 showing police inviting people into the building. Capitol security video also shows police waiving people into the building. The new speaker of the House Kevin McCarthy gave this previously suppressed video to Tucker Carlson on February 28, 2023. The Capitol Police report to Pelosi. They would not have invited Trump supporters into the building on their own, without authorization. They would have been fired if they had.

Democrat Congresswoman AOC, aka Alexandria Ocasio-Cortez, strongly complained in a video about how the Capitol Police had invited Trump supporters into the building, and had socialized and chit-chatted with the protesters, and had made no attempt to remove them. She said she felt threatened in the building after January 6 because she felt the videos showed that the Capitol Police would not giving adequate protection for her. So here is a Democrat who despises Trump acknowledging that the police enticed people into the building and then did not kick them out. Pelosi then instructed AOC to shut up about the police behavior. We have not heard any further complaints

---

[12] NBC News, February 2, 2023.

from her, even though she had been extremely upset and worried,

* * *

Sean Hannity has shown on his show hundreds of times a video of a Capitol Police officer standing by a four foot high metal barrier about 50 yards from the building that was intended to keep the protesters away from the building. The barrier looks almost like a high bike rack. The officer swings the barrier open so that there is a 20 foot gap, and she stands next to the gap waiving people into the restricted area leading to the building. The officer appears to be a woman about 5 foot 5 inches tall with a slightly plump body. Hannity has asked many times why she has not been identified. She should be interviewed to find out who authorized her to open the gate and waive people in. Surely she would have been fired if she had done this on her own, without orders. And then investigators could ask the police brass *why* they instructed the officer to waive the Trump supporters in, and who higher up instructed them to give the order. Possibly all the way up to Pelosi.

* * *

There are videos of the infamous horned guy, Jacob Chansley, standing in one of the smaller rotunda politely talking to a few police officers. They advise him to be peaceful. They do not ask him to leave the room or the building. Jacob then yells to the crowd, "We must be peaceful. Do not destroy any property. We have the right to assemble under the constitution." He never gets into an argument with the police in the video nor in any other videos.

Chansley, the horned guy, then leaves the small rotunda, and he appears in another video as he enters a smaller, stately Senate hearing room. He is escorted by a Capitol Police officer, and the two treat each other with courtesy and respect. Chansley says hello to two protesters who are sitting on the floor looking at their cell phones, and then he walks up to the podium and sits in the chairperson's chair. The officer tells him that's inappropriate, and Chansley immediately stands up and gets off the podium. There is no violence. There is no property damage.

The newly released (February 2023) Capitol security video to Tucker Carlson shows many minutes of Chansley. In NONE of the videos did he harm or threaten anyone, or harm any property. He shows politeness to the police, and reverence to the building and it's artwork.

Despite having committed no violence, damaged no property, and been respectful to the police, the deranged judge in Chansley's case sentenced Chansley to 41 months in prison. The idiot, that is the judge, explained at sentencing that even though Chansley had done nothing egregious and had essentially only trespassed (maybe not — did the police let him into the building, thus waiving the trespass charge?), that because of all the publicity Chansley had received, the judge thought Chansley was the "face of the protest," and so should receive a severe sentence, to "set an example." Are you kidding? What horrible logic. A judge like that should be banned for life from the judiciary, and disbarred from the practice of law. He has absolutely no sense of justice or fairness. All he cares about is the Washington DC cocktail parties he and his wife would not get invited to if he had issued a lighter, fairer sentence. He is the Swamp personified. He is scum. He is why the trust in the judiciary has had a record low according to several polls. The ruling elite cannot be trusted.

* * *

In the video of Ashli Babbitt, just before she was shot by a Capitol Police 'officer', Ashli is standing about eight feet from three Capitol Policemen guarding a windowed set of doors leading to an inner area, the Speaker's Lobby. None of the three make any effort to move the protesters away from the doors. The officers watch the protesters, and there is no conflict between the two groups. The officers talk to the protesters in what appears to be a friendly conversation. There also is a single officer holding a rifle a little bit behind Ashli. He just watches the crowd. This again shows that the police were instructed by superiors, going up to the top, to Pelosi possibly, to not quell breaches into the building.

The three officers then do something odd. One of them makes eye contact with someone out of the video, and makes a quick hand signal. Then they leave their guard station in front of the doors, and are not seen in the video again. No one is guarding the doors from the outside after that. Whoever directed the three officers to leave appears to have wanted the protesters, or maybe FBI informants, to attack the doors.

A crazed man wearing black glasses then starts smashing the glass. Ashli tries to stop him, and punches the man in the side of his head. You can see his glasses get half-way knocked off. He pushes her away, and destroys the window. She then jumps into the window frame, and officer Michael Byrd shoots her, and murders her.

The entire Ashli Babbitt video shows a Capitol Police force that does not care much about protecting the building, and actually wants to allow protesters to be drawn inside the building more so that people like Byrd can murder them, or so FBI informants can abuse them. Again, the Capitol Police report to Pelosi. More admissible evidence to support a jury guilty verdict or civil jury finding against Pelosi.

* * *

There are many other videos shot by eye witnesses showing the Capitol Police interacting with the protesters in a friendly manner, and essentially telling the protesters, 'Yes, this is a public building, you are invited in, and we will not kick you out. This is "The People's Building."' For example, there are several videos showing protesters walking through a giant public portion of the building, The Capitol Rotunda. The interesting thing about the videos is there is a tourist walking area, about six feet wide, that is bordered by silk ropes, like those used in a movie theater. There is nothing to prevent a person from ducking under the silk ropes, and walking throughout the room. But none of the hundreds of protesters ducks under the ropes to wander the room. They all walk peacefully between the ropes, two by two, looking at the splendor of the room, snapping pictures. No one wandered around the room outside of the ropes.

There are other videos showing police standing at entrances to the building, holding the doors open for the protesters to let them in, like New York City doormen. Then the police stood with their backs to the walls in the long hallways, just watching the people walk by, not stopping anybody. The police, through their behavior, were telling people that the building was open to the public, as it often is.

Thus, the police guarding the building created an inviting atmosphere at the entrances and inside, telling the protesters "that it was OK to enter and wander around. They would not be trespassing nor charged with trespass." Entrapment. Pelosi's entrapment. Boy, were the protesters gamed. Garland's army of psychopathic goon prosecutors, and Christopher Wray's army of unbalanced, fascist agents would later persecute these poor people like Stalin terrorized the bourgeoisie.

* * *

Rep. Marjorie Taylor Greene (R-GA) is arguing that Pelosi is directly responsible for failed security measures and should be held responsible for her actions.

In a tweet, Rep. Marjorie Taylor Greene (R-GA) said, "Nancy Pelosi is directly to blame for the security failures at the Capitol on January

6th. She blamed everyone else now she must pay the price."

However, Pelosi's deputy chief of staff, Drew Hammil, argued against Greene's claims, saying that the Republican is spreading "lies."

"More lies. More threats of political violence. Where is Kevin McCarthy? He's groveling to this extreme MAGA element of his party to become the weakest Speaker of the House in history," Hammill tweeted in response.

To back up her claims, Greene cited a scathing report from House Republicans that contain emails and text messages, exposing the truth that Pelosi was involved in security measures for that day.

"Then-House Sergeant at Arms Paul Irving — who served on the Capitol Police Board by virtue of his position — succumbed to political pressures from the Office of Speaker Pelosi and House Democrat leadership leading up to January 6, 2021," the report read, adding "he coordinated closely with the Speaker and her staff and left Republicans out of important discussions related to security."

Irving reportedly "coordinated closely" with Pelosi and her staff on security plans for Jan. 6, however, Republicans were purposely left out of "important discussions related to security."

He argued that Pelosi and House Democrats were "compromised by politics and did not adequately prepare for violence at the Capitol."

The report, which was released by Jim Banks (R-IN), Jim Jordan (R-OH), Rodney Davis (R-IL), Kelly Armstrong (R-ND), and Troy Nehls (R-TX), said that "the Speaker's office was heavily involved in planning and decision-making before and during the events of Jan. 6, 2021, and micromanaged the Sergeant at Arms."

Despite Pelosi continually saying she "has no power over the Capitol Police," the outgoing House Speaker spoke to Irving 36 times about Capitol security and attended meetings in December 2020 leading up to the protests. [13]

John Solomon, an investigative reporter stated on Fox News' Sean Hannity Show on Dec 21, 2022: "Five Republicans including Jim Jordan got the emails between Pelosi's staff and the security staff at the Capitol police. Pelosi had said on February 29, 2021 that "I could not have influenced the security of the Capitol police, I have no power over the Capitol police." This was a lie. The emails and texts show just the opposite. Pelosi and her staff were directly involved in meeting with the Capitol police and the security planners and the House sergeant of arms going back to early December 2020. She and her staff had multiple meetings. Her staff was actually editing some of the security plans on January 5. Which means that the opportunity to prevent the entering the Capitol was not just a failure of the Capitol Police, it was the failure of the political leadership of Pelosi and her leaders."

* * *

Of course, not all the Capitol Police officers let protesters into the building. Many actually did guard the entrances and windows, and fight with the protesters. However, many officers lost their minds with their anger, hatred and intolerance for Trump supporters (so much for the 'tolerant and open-minded' myth of the liberal populace of Washington DC). Some of the police were extremely violent even though unprovoked, and they likely killed at least three protesters. Why the police, as shown in the videos, were inviting to the protesters at some entrances, but blocking other entrances and fighting with the protesters at those other doors is unclear. Perhaps the police were inviting to the people at those doors that were normally open to the public, but not at the doors the were normally private. It's a mystery.

Hundreds have entered the building. Video shows Jacob Chansley,

---

[13] Sarah Arnold

the so-called "QAnon shaman," and a few protesters talking calmly with Capitol Police officers.10 Rather than telling them to leave, the officers tell Chansley's group they must behave. Officer Keith Robishaw tells Chansley's group they won't stop them from entering. "We're not against . . . you need to show us . . . no attacking, no assault, remain calm," Robishaw can be heard saying in an open-source video. Chansley agrees. "This has to be peaceful," Chansley yells to the others. "We have the right to peacefully assemble." Shirtless and .... Kelly

"The US Capitol Police is hiding a reported 14,000 hours of January 6 video from the American people to help Nancy Pelosi's abusive targeting of Trump supporters and other political opponents," Judicial Watch President Tom Fitton said in a press release responding to the filing. "Any other police department in America would be investigated and defunded for such abusive secrecy. The Pelosi Congress is in cover-up mode regarding January 6."

Would the videos indeed show officers allowing people into the building, as plenty of open source videos showed, or reveal that most of the protesters were peaceful and unaware they were committing any crime? The videos have just been released (February 2023).

There is security video showing people inside the building, before the breach, opening up the giant metal Columbus Ave doors, that can only be opened with a code to the electric lock. This allowed the protesters to enter through that doorway.

The videos explained why the Justice Department is working so hard to keep the footage secret. One clip shows dozens of people casually entering an open door on the Senate wing of the building at around 2:25 p.m. as others climb through an open, perhaps previously broken, large window. Police are absent.

Benny Thompson the chairman of the committee said Pelosi's records were off the table. Her emails, her communications, anything related to Jan 6. Same with capitol police emails.

Liz Cheney had her hand in on preventing proper security. She wanted the breach to occur so she could take out her main Republican rival. About a week before January 6, Cheney, who is aligned with Pelosi, threated any National Guard commanders with arrest if they went to the Capitol to protect it. She cited some vague, obscure federal statute. She made the threat in an opinion piece in the Dem operated Washington Post. She then later tried to take out Trump by manipulating, doctoring and hiding the evidence that the January 6 committee collected. She doesn't believe in the rule of law. She allowed hearsay testimony (Hutchinson), didn't allow cross-examination, hid exculpatory evidence, and hid Pelosi's emails and texts.

Anyone who threatened or attacked police officers, or caused property damage should be prosecuted under our normal standards of justice, including all FBI agents and informants who threatened, encouraged, attacked or destroyed property. Protesters should not be persecuted like Putin's political prisoners, as Attorney General Garland has done, and held in pre-trial detention for 2 years, some in solitary confinement without medical treatment. They should be released on bail pending their trials as is common in our judicial system. Prosecutors should provide all exculpatory evidence as required under our constitution. Prosecutors have failed to do so, and they should be fired, permanently lose their law licenses and pensions, and be liable for civil damages, without any government indemnification, since their actions were reckless. This punishment should also be doled out to Merrick Garland who has authorized this bizarre persecution. No one who was waived or tacitly invited into the building by the police should be arrested or prosecuted for any reason. But yes, protesters who broke the law should be fairly prosecuted.

Compare how the Jan 6 protesters are being treated compared to the true insurrectionists, those violent far left-wing thugs who murdered and burned during the BLM protests in the summer of 2020. They tried to burn down a courthouse in Portland full of federal police for over a month, and assaulted federal police, and then the DOJ later dropped almost all charges. Their efforts amounted to attempted murder. Garland, why did you drop these charges, but throw 67 year old grandmothers in prison for months for simply taking pictures of the architecture inside the Capitol

THE FBI'S ATTACK ON THE CAPITOL BUILDING & CONNECTION TO PELOSI AS EVIDENCE OF HER GUILT

Why is the FBI's role in January 6 relevant to whether or not Pelosi would likely or not be found guilty or liable by a jury for the breach of the Capitol Building on January 6? Two things must be shown to connect the FBI to Pelosi. First, it must be shown what the FBI did, if anything, to encourage or enable the breach of the building. Second, it must be shown that the FBI was aligned with the Democrat Party, and therefore with Pelosi. If these two assertions can be proven, then they would constitute circumstantial evidence of her guilt and liability. As was stated in a prior chapter, circumstantial evidence is just as valuable as direct evidence in a court of law.

* * *

The FBI was instrumental in causing and enabling the breach of the Capitol Building

It's still unclear how many undercover FBI agents or informants were involved, and we may never know. Requests for documents, videos, and email exchanges between top officials have been denied.

In October 2022 The New York Times reported there were 20 federal assets in the Oath Keepers and 8 in the Proud Boys. Why did they not stop the violence at the Capitol? Were they violent themselves?

"At least one FBI informant was later revealed to have been in the group of Proud Boys. The informant would remain in constant contact with his FBI handler about the group's activity that day. Ethan Nordean, also known as Rufio Panman, is wearing all black, a pair of dark sunglasses, and using a bullhorn to corral the group behind him. "Proud Boys," Nordean randomly says into the bullhorn at one point. [14]"

There is video showing that the first people through the windows into a large rotunda room were dressed like FBI agents undercover agents. They wore all black. No Trump supporter dresses like that. Look at the Trump supporters in the crowd and at rallies. None like that. Their faces were covered (no Trump supporters had their faces covered). They acted methodically in breaking the windows and expertly jumping through the windows. Once through, no one arrested them!

The FBI had agents dressed like Trump supporters, wearing red Trump hats *inside* the Capitol Building *before* the building was breached from the outside by FBI agents, undercover DC Police, and protesters. The head of the FBI, Christopher Wray, admitted this during Congressional testimony in January 2023. The Congressman asked Wray, "Did you have FBI agents dressed like Trump supporters inside the building before the building was breached?" Wray should have answered, "No." Instead he said, "It would not be proper for me to answer that question." Of course he could answer that question if the answer was "No!" He would have said "No!!" Why not? He would not be disclosing any FBI 'methods' if he said "No." Wray's answer was absurd. His answer should have been "No." So the FBI *must have had* agents dressed like Trump supporters inside the building *before* people broke into the Capitol Building. It's *irrefutable.*

The FBI admits their informants were violent at Jan 6

The FBI admitted they had informants at the Jan 6 protest who

---

[14] Julie Kelly, *January 6: How the Democrats Used The Capitol Protest To Launch A War of Terror On the Political Right* (New York: Post Hill Press, 2022), ch 8, loc 2980.

committed violent act against the Capitol police. At a Senate hearing in February 2022 Senator Ted Cruz asked the FBI senior official, "Did the FBI have informants at the Jan 6 protest at the Capitol who committed violent acts against the Capitol police?" The FBI official said, "Sir, I am not in a position to answer that." So, the official would have said "No" if in fact no FBI informant committed violent acts. The FBI would be disclosing no 'secret' information, nor revealing 'methods of operation' if she had said "No." There is no logical nor good reason not to say "No" if that is true. So obviously the FBI had agents who were committing violent acts at the Capitol on Jan 6.

FBI agents posed as Trump supporters at Jan 6

DOJ head Garland testified to Congress that FBI agents posed as Trump supporters at the Jan 6 protest, but he refused to say how many. Oct 21, 2021. Garland also stated that the FBI *always* and routinely has agents and informants at major political rallies like Trump rally, a *mile* from the Capitol Building.

An Oath Keeper defense lawyer Brad Geiger identified 80 suspicious actors who have not been arrested or charged, identified. They were present in concentrations where there was trouble. Lib sedition hunters have given all 80 numbers. They worked in 2 man teams. They were later seen on the terrace. The prosecutors won't comment about this. They were at the first breach point. Then they were at the steps. About 20 were where Ashli shot.

Ray Epps told protesters 'we need to go into the Capitol,' and he was never charged Others people were charge for telling people to go into the Capitol. Epps denied being an informant. He is seen before Trump finished his rally. Epps was at breach point 1 and 2.

There is a video showing the Columbus doors to the building and suspicious actors holding the inner door open with a wooden pole, and pushing people in.

There is a video showing another guy encouraging people to enter.

There is a video showing a guy breaking a window with a club. A Trump guy stops him. 4 guys attack the Trump guy. A lady witness also stops the club guy. They tackle her. The FBI guy with the bull horn points at her and yells 'get her out of here.'

The Oath Keepers are the center for the prosecutors. But video shows them helping the police. Cop asks them for help. They help 16 cops leave. They were charged with seditious conspiracy. They did not bring weapons. They had weapons stoed in Virginia. A 2nd helped a cop. A 3rd guarded a window.[15]

"This would imply that elements of the federal government were active instigators in the most egregious and spectacular aspects of 1/6, amounting to a monumental entrapment scheme used as a pretext to imprison otherwise harmless protesters at the Capitol—and in a much larger sense used to frame the entire MAGA movement as potential domestic terrorists. Given the FBI's long history of using false-front groups as flypaper to attract dangerous radicals, and then moving them to commit actionable crimes, this kind of speculation seems far from unreasonable. Julie Kelly

Julie Kelly:

"As it turns out, Epps is more than a retired Marine who loves his country. He also is the former head of the Arizona chapter of the Oath Keepers, the group still run by Stewart Rhodes. They are photographed together at various events in 2011.

"A few days after Beattie's piece was posted, Attorney General Merrick Garland testified before the House Judiciary Committee. Rep. Tom Massie played a video montage of Epps' clips from January 5 and

---

[15] Epoch Times' video, "The Real Story Jan 6"

6 and challenged Garland to explain them.

* * *

"Massie: 'I was hoping today to give you an opportunity to put to rest the concerns that people have that there were federal agents or assets of the federal government present on January 5 and January 6. Can you tell us, without talking about particular incidents or particular videos, how many agents or assets of the federal government were present on January 6, whether they agitated to go into the Capitol, and if any of them did?' Garland: 'So I'm not going to violate this norm of, of, of, the rule of law.'

"Inconsistencies are also appearing in the prosecution of the Proud Boys. Enrique Tarrio, the head of the group, was arrested on January 4 in Washington on an outstanding warrant for burning a BLM flag.

"The timing of his arrest, which prevented him from joining a large group of Proud Boys on January 6, and the fact he had not been named in any Proud Boy indictment led to speculation he might be working with the feds. After all, he had done so before. A January 2021 report by Reuters revealed that Tarrio had a history as a government informant. "A Federal Bureau of Investigation agent and Tarrio's own lawyer described his undercover work and said he had helped authorities prosecute more than a dozen people in various cases involving drugs, gambling and human smuggling,' Aram Roston disclosed in the January 27 article. "The records uncovered by Reuters are startling because they show that a leader of a far-right group now under intense scrutiny by law enforcement was previously an active collaborator with criminal investigators." Tarrio's cooperation with the government came after he was charged in 2012 for fraud. When asked for comment, Tarrio told Roston he didn't "recall any of this."

* * *

"Then came a bombshell from the New York Times: the group of Proud Boys in the capitol on January 6 included at least two federal informants who were in constant communication with their FBI handlers. "The informant, who started working with the F.B.I. in July 2020, appears to have been close to several other members of his Proud Boys chapter, including some who have been charged in the attack," Alan Feuer wrote on September 25. The Times had received access to confidential records documenting the informants' activities.

"Aside from the revelation about FBI informants within the Proud Boys during the Capitol protest, Feuer also suggested that the information did not prove the Proud Boys conspired to "stop, delay, or hinder Congress' certification of the Electoral College vote," as the government alleged in indictments. The informant, according to the documents Feuer viewed, repeatedly said the Proud Boys' plan was to maintain a defensive posture and prepare to fight leftist agitators such as Antifa. A few weeks later, Feuer followed up with an article over a dispute between Joe Biggs, the Proud Boys leader on the ground that day, and Ryan Samsel, one of the first protesters to knock down barriers

"Biggs also had a relationship with the FBI. He turned himself in to two agents, including "one he'd known for a long time," according to his lawyer, on January 20. In a court filing, Biggs' lawyers described how his client routinely met and spoke with the FBI, including agents at the Portland FBI field office, about his plans to organize Proud Boys rallies in that city as a counter demonstration to Antifa protests. In 2018, FBI agents in Florida, where Biggs lives, started questioning "what Biggs meant by something politically or culturally provocative he had said on the air or on social media concerning a national issue, political parties, the Proud Boys, Antifa or other groups," his lawyer wrote.

"Coincidentally—or perhaps not—D'Antuono, the FBI brass

whom Wray moved from the Detroit field office to Washington, D.C. just a few weeks before the election, promised a scorched earth approach. "Just because you've left the D.C. region, you can still expect a knock on the door if we find out that you were part of criminal activity inside the Capitol. Bottom line—the FBI is not sparing any resources in this investigation," D'Antuono said in a January 8 statement.[16]"

Obviously FBI 'agent' D'Antuono is a threat to our country, our democracy and our constitution. Is he a Putin stooge taking bribes to disrupt us and divide us? Who knows. But he clearly is not fit to be a dog catcher in a small town, and he should be in prison for obstruction of justice.

---

[16] Julie Kelly, *January 6: How the Democrats Used The Capitol Protest To Launch A War of Terror On the Political Right* (New York: Post Hill Press, 2022), ch 8, loc 3590.

DC METROPOLITAN UNDERCOVER POLICE INSTIGATE THE VIOLENCE

DC Metropolitan Police helped to instigate the breach of the Capitol Building as detailed in the following article. The DC police on the one hand politely invited people into the building, and on the other hand savagely beat people. The DC Police are part of the DC Democrat Machine which in turn coordinates with Pelosi's Democrat mafia. Also, the DC Police coordinated with the Capitol Police, and do so on a regular basis. Thus, this is more circumstantial evidence implicating Pelosi that a jury could consider in evaluating her guilt or liability.

*   *   *

From the Epoch Times, as footnoted:

"Three D.C. Metropolitan Police Department undercover officers acted as provocateurs at the northwest steps of the U.S. Capitol on Jan. 6, 2021, a federal prosecutor admitted in court papers.

"The admission came in a March 24 filing before U.S. District Judge Rudolph Contreras that seeks to keep video footage shot by the officers under court seal.

"Prosecutors accused the defendant in the case—William Pope of Topeka, Kansas—of an "illegitimate" attempt to unmask the video as part of his alleged strategy to try the case in the news media. Pope filed a motion to remove the court seal on Feb. 21.

""The defendant is not entitled to 'undesignate' these videos to share them with unlimited third parties," Assistant U.S. Attorney Kelly Moran said. "His desire to try his case in the media rather than in a court of law is illegitimate, and the government has met its burden to show the necessity of the protective order."

"Video footage long hidden under court seal has become a major topic, especially with prosecutors disclosing the involvement of multiple FBI informants in a number of high-profile Jan. 6 cases.

"Pope is seeking to lift the court seal on the undercover video toward obtaining full access to video evidence held by the government. Pope is representing himself in the criminal case being prosecuted against him. At a hearing on March 3, 2023 Contreras seemed sympathetic to Pope's motion to unmask the videos.

"The officer clearly incited that area, and we still don't have video from all other undercover MPD," Pope told The Epoch Times. "And as the numerous informants in the Proud Boys trial demonstrates, we are only just beginning to scratch the surface on FBI involvement."

"The undercover video footage—a portion of which was posted on Rumble on March 24—shows three members of the MPD's Electronic Surveillance Unit approaching the Capitol's northwest steps. One of the men, while surveying the crowd, states, "Someone's going to get shot."

"Officer 2 replies, "They're not going to shoot anybody."

"Along the edge of the Capitol property, Officer 2 encourages one protester to go up to the building.

""Go join 'em then," he says. The man replies, "No, I've got my bike to guard."

"The men engage in banter on the walk across the west Capitol lawn.

"'Never Seen Anything Like This'

""This is amazing," Officer 2 says. Officer 1, who was recording the GoPro video, replies, "Yeah, I've never seen anything like this."

"Nearly 30 members of the Electronic Surveillance Unit were assigned to duty on Jan. 6, 2021, some of whom were gathering evidence on crowd activity. Members wore special bands on their left wrists to identify themselves as part of the unit, according to the MPD's 96-page Jan. 6 action plan.

"Officer 1 repeatedly joins in chants of "Drain the swamp!" and

"Our house! Our house! Our house!"

""A little closer to the Capitol, the video footage captures a protester shouting: "Joe Biden! We wanna hear you speak, you [expletive] pedophile satanist [expletive]!"

"A short time later, Officer 1 joins the crowd in a "USA!" chant, repeating the phrase five times.

"At the foot of the northwest stairs, someone leans part of a bicycle rack against the balustrade. As a protester climbs up the makeshift ladder, Officer 1 shouts: "C'mon, man, let's go! Leave that [expletive]."

"Officer 1 gets help from a protester climbing onto the balustrade of the steps. Then, surveying the people moving up the staircase, he shouts, "C'mon, go, go, go!"

"Officer 1 encourages the crowd to move up the stairs with repeated shouts of "Keep going!"

"Once Officer 1 jumps from the balustrade onto the stairs, he passes someone he knew, a man in a blue sweatshirt who was wearing a dark cap, protective goggles, and what appears to be a Halloween mask.

""Tim!" the officer says, to which the unidentified man replies, "What's going on, bro?"

""Walking on a sidewalk next to the Capitol, Officer 1 hears a protester say, "Now they're letting everybody in, there ain't nowhere to go."

"Officer 1 replies, "I think it's going to … they're going to trap everyone in."

""This video clearly evidences undercover law enforcement officers urging the crowds to advance up the stairs and scaffolding towards the Capitol on January 6," Pope wrote in an earlier case filing. "The government may claim that incidents like this did not happen, but the facts show they did."

"Moran, the prosecutor, acknowledges such in a motion filed on

March 24, 2023.

""The specific footage, GoPro video recorded by an MPD police officer who was stationed at the Capitol in an evidence-gathering capacity, captures the officer shouting words to the effect of, "Go! Go! Go!" Moran wrote.

""At other times in these videos, the officer and the two other plainclothes officers with him appear to join the crowd around them in various chants, including "drain the swamp," "U.S.A.! U.S.A.! U.S.A.!", and "Whose house? Our house!"

"Moran also argued against unsealing large amounts of closed-circuit television (CCTV) security video, which she said could put officers at risk.

""There are very specific and highly worrisome risks associated with the specific videos the defendant seeks to share en masse," she wrote.

""Given the highly volatile nature of the discourse surrounding these cases, releasing the identities of the officers depicted in these videos—officers the defendant now claims to have instigated the entire attack on the U.S. Capitol—would surely put the lives of those officers at risk."

"Pope told The Epoch Times that he never made such a claim. He hasn't yet filed a response to the government's memorandum.

"Another video that Pope discovered in his research shows Officer 2 and Officer 3 walking behind Ashli Babbitt on the northwest steps. About an hour later, Babbitt was shot at the entry of the Speaker's Lobby by Capitol Police Lt. Michael Byrd. She died a half-hour later.[17]"

*　　*　　*

From The Epoch Times as footnoted.

---

[17] Joseph M Hanneman, "Prosecutor admit DC police officers acted as provocateurs at US Capitol on Jan 6," *The Epoch Times*, March 24, 2023.

"Just minutes after misfired tear gas canisters drove police back into the U.S. Capitol on Jan. 6, 2021, the retreating officers left unsecured the sets of double doors in the Lower West Terrace tunnel, giving protesters easy access to the entrance and sparking several hours of brutal violence, videos reveal.

"Cell phone video entered into evidence in a recent Jan. 6 criminal case shows that protesters walked right through the sets of double doors at the back of the tunnel and began fighting against the police for access to the rest of the Capitol.

""For months, questions have been raised by defense attorneys and case observers whether the doors at the tunnel entrance were locked and secure. Prosecutors contended in court filings that the doors were locked when the last officers retreated into the Capitol at about 2:40 p.m.

"However, two videos that were entered into evidence by the U.S. Department of Justice in Jan. 6 criminal cases show that neither set of doors was secured. All protesters had to do was pull on the outer handles to gain entry.

"The easy defeat of the tunnel doors led to more than two hours of the worst violence recorded at the Capitol on Jan. 6.

"It led to the death of Rosanne Boyland, 34, who was trampled by the crowd after police deployed gas in the tunnel, and was later beaten by an MPD officer armed with a walking stick.

"The tunnel was also where Jan. 6 defendant Victoria White was beaten by Bagshaw and other officers with expandable steel batons and fists.

"The first people to confront the police line after Mehaffie opened the inner door used flagpoles to stab at officers, who blocked the inner hallway with shields.

"One protester, possibly Mehaffie, shouted, "Don't hurt the police! Don't hurt the police! Don't hurt the police! Don't hurt them!""[18]

*　　*　　*

From the Epoch Times, as footnoted:

"Three undercover Metropolitan Police Department officers joined the march of protesters up the northwest side of the Capitol on Jan. 6, 2021—including one who climbed over a barricade and pushed others toward the Capitol, and another who walked behind Ashli Babbitt and predicted that "someone will get shot," according to newly disclosed court documents.

"New court motions filed by Jan. 6 defendant William Pope of Topeka, Kansas, also show MPD bicycle officers stopping four armed men in plainclothes on Jan. 6. The men turned out to be federal agents. Video included with Pope's filings also shows uniformed MPD officers saying, "we were set up" to fail on Jan. 6.

"Information in the court papers will rekindle the debate about the role that undercover officers and agents played in the riots of Jan. 6 and why the U.S. Department of Justice and federal judges have kept the evidence under seal and away from public view.

""This video clearly evidences undercover law enforcement officers urging the crowds to advance up the stairs and scaffolding towards the Capitol on January 6," Pope wrote in one motion. "The government may claim that incidents like this did not happen, but the facts show they did.

""Since the government cannot be trusted to disclose these facts," Pope wrote, "it becomes even more important that defense teams, including Pro Se defendants, be able to directly examine the evidence."

---

[18] Joseph M Hanneman, "Police left lower west terrace tunnel doors unsecured, giving protesters easy access," *The Epoch Times, March 31,* 2023.

* * *

"The three undercover MPD officers approached the northwest corner of the Capitol grounds at about 1:40 p.m. on Jan. 6, one of the motions states. Officer 1, who was filming their journey, joined the crowd chanting, "Drain the swamp!"

"When a group of men ran past them toward the Capitol, Officer 2 —wearing a Trump beanie—remarked, "Those guys are getting shot," the motion said.

"At the base of the scaffold stairs, Officer 1 joined the crowd in a chant, "Whose house? Our house!"

""Officer 1 began yelling at people in front of him to 'Go, go, go!' As they climbed bicycle racks, Officer 1 yelled for the crowd to 'help him up, help him up!" followed by 'push him up, push him up!'" the motion reads of Pope describing how Officer 1 climbed over a barricade.

""Needing help to get up, Officer 1 asked a nearby man to give him a boost," the motion says. "The man gives Officer 1 a lift up, and Officer 1 says 'Thanks, bro.'"

"Officer 1 pushed protesters in front of him to advance on the Capitol, shouting, "c'mon, c'mon, c'mon, let's go!," the motion said. People around him climbed over bike-rack-style barricades and scaffolding that had been set up for the presidential inauguration.

Right Behind Ashli Babbitt

"At one point, Officers 2 and 3 were almost directly behind Trump supporter Ashli Babbitt on the exterior stairs, about an hour before Babbitt was gunned down at the entrance to the Speaker's Lobby, Pope said in a Twitter post on Feb. 18.

""Why hasn't the government informed the public that undercover MPD officers were chanting, 'Our house!' and repeatedly urging protesters to advance up the northwest steps of the Capitol on January 6?" Pope wrote on Twitter under his handle @FreeStateWill. "Officer 2 said someone would get shot and went up right behind Ashli Babbitt."

"Video shot by the undercover officers is under court seal.

"Pope argued in his motions that the DOJ is trying to prevent him from accessing the full Jan. 6 evidence databases. He is defending himself against seven criminal counts brought by federal prosecutors in February 2021. He asked U.S. District Judge Rudolph Contreras to compel the DOJ to give him full access to discovery materials.

"In a motion filed with the court on Feb. 17, Pope included a tranche of bodycam video with evidence not disclosed publicly before.

"The bodycams of three MPD bicycle officers—Tyquan Brown, Daniel Styles, and Christopher Vanacore—shows them stopping a group of four men and a woman at 12:19 p.m., walking east during then-President Trump's speech at the Ellipse. "Is anyone armed?" Brown asked. "We all are," the men said, adding that they were law enforcement officials. The woman was not armed.

"The four men showed the MPD officers their law-enforcement credentials and were allowed to go on their way. The IDs all appeared very similar, but the video is not of sufficient resolution to read what agency they are from. Brown chided one of the men, "You've got to do a little bit better at hiding it," pointing to his concealed handgun.

"The bodycam of MPD Officer Lawrence Lazewski shows Lazewski and another MPD officer express the belief that police had been "set up" on Jan. 6.

"After nearly 90 minutes on the police line on the west front of the Capitol, Lazewski retreated to the Upper West Terrace at 2:33 p.m. He approached a group of other officers, one of whom was engaged in an animated discussion.

'They Set Us Up'

""They set us the [expletive] up," the officer said. "That's what they did. They set us up.

""They set up [Unit] 64, absolutely, and then they ask you all to come two hours later," the officer said. "They set us up."

"Lazewski replied, "They needed everybody right away," to which the other officer said, "Nah, right away, they set us the [expletive] up. We ain't got [expletive]."

"A few moments later, the unidentified officer said, "Take this mother[expletive]," and waved his hand at the Capitol in disgust.

"At about 2:40 p.m., half an hour after the Capitol was first breached, Lazewski who was outside the building approached another MPD officer on the side of the Capitol. On the way, he heard a group of officers discussing the police deployment of CS gas along the barricades on the west front. Many officers were not outfitted with gas masks.

""I didn't know we were coming up for this or I would have made sure we all had our masks," the officer told Lazewski.

""I didn't realize how bad … they set us up to fail," Lazewski said.

""They did," the other officer replied.

""There was no way we were winning that," Lazewski said. "Now you've got at least four platoons that are just gassed out."

'Keep the March Going'

"Video from the bodycam of MPD Officer Terry Thorne shows him imploring protesters on the way down Constitution Avenue to the Capitol from Trump's speech at 12:30 p.m. to "keep the march going."

""Let's keep it going," Thorne said, waving protesters away from a side street. "Let's keep the march going. Let's keep it going. Guys, let's keep the march going."

""Bodycam from MPD Officer Anthony Alioto gives a behind the scenes look at police action along the west front of the Capitol. His bodycam captured some of the actions of Officer Daniel Thau, who used a taser on protesters four times, tossed countless munitions into the crowd, and fired a 40 mm shell at protesters.

""On Alioto's video, Thau is shown using pepper spray on protesters that is partially blown back in officers' faces. "Hey Danny," Alioto said. "Watch the wind direction!"

""Officer Luke Foskett's bodycam shows some of the chaos inside the Capitol. He approached a Capitol Police supervisor and asked, "Where can we start?"

""I don't [expletive] know," the man replied. "You want to talk about getting caught with your pants down. We have no direction. Nobody can get on the [expletive] radio.

""I called the Command Center and let them know that you guys are here with us. At least you're accounted for," the Capitol officer said.

"Officers in that section of the Capitol were looking for a man who might have been armed. Someone asked the Capitol Police supervisor how they could identify undercover operatives.

""They will have a wristband. Their guns will have a candy stripe on the barrel," he said. "I don't know the wristband color but they'll have a wristband somewhere.""[19]

*　　*　　*

From Julie Kellie and her review of hours of video footage:

In a video Michael Byrd, a U.S. Capitol Police officer, instructs members on the House side to look under their seats for a packaged gas mask. "Please grab a mask and place it on your lap," Byrd said. "And be prepared to don your mask in the event we have a breach." It

---

[19] Joseph M Hanneman, "Undercover DC Police Officer Pushed Protesters, Toward Capitol, Climbed Over Police Barricade: Court Filing," *The Epoch Times*, February 19, 2023.

is unclear why gas masks were placed ahead of time in the Chamber.

"The police shot "flashbangs" into a large crowd outside the building on the west side. The crowd, which is not at this time attempting to breach the barriers, includes young children and senior citizens, according to witnesses. What happens next by all accounts is unprovoked and leads to a sharp escalation of anger and violence. Trump supporters uninvolved with the initial breach or skirmishes with police are shocked to find themselves assaulted by law enforcement. Unlike the mild-mannered officers seen on the perimeter of the grounds or inside, US Capitol and D.C. Metro police guarding the building are covered head to toe in helmets, gas masks, and boots. Michael Bolton, the USCP inspector general, later confirmed that D.C. Metro officers used sting balls. "They're very painful, these types of munitions," Bolton told Congress in April. A sting ball is a hand-held grenade that produces a loud sound, a bright flash of light, and a blast of approximately 180 rubber pellets with a radius of up to fifty feet. Police also used what one judge later described as "super soakers" filled with tear gas.

"An officer fired a teargas canister—not at the plainclothes militants at the front line, but into the crowd itself. Then another. Flash grenades went off in the middle of the crowd. The tear gas caused pandemonium. But there was still no stampede, and people helped create or widen paths to allow others to leave the area. Some, seeing frail or elderly people who had a hard time standing, broke into a pallet of black folding chairs for the inauguration and distributed them.

"Video shows Jacob Chansley, the so-called "QAnon shaman," and a few protesters talking calmly with Capitol Police officers. Rather than telling them to leave, the officers tell Chansley's group they must behave. Officer Keith Robishaw tells Chansley's group they won't stop them from entering. "We're not against . . . you need to show us . . . no attacking, no assault, remain calm," Robishaw can be heard saying in an open-source video. Chansley agrees. "This has to be peaceful," Chansley yells to the others. "We have the right to peacefully assemble."

"Besides the political persecution of Trump supporters post Jan 6 that the above DC Police actions caused, one of the saddest aspects arising from the above is that prosecutors and judges, in serious violation of their ethical rules and duties, hid this exculpatory evidence. They should all be fired or impeached, and lose their pensions and health care, and if possible be sued in civil court, and hopefully lose, and then have all their assets taken by the plaintiffs, the victims, as compensation.

"The Capitol police let people in to the building as shown on surveillance video, and they also attacked the crowd. The police used flash bangs, rubber bullets, tear gas and non lethal weapons to inflame the crowd.[20]"

---

[20] Julie Kelly, *January 6: How the Democrats Used The Capitol Protest To Launch A War of Terror On the Political Right* (New York: Post Hill Press, 2022), ch 1.

THE FBI IS ALLIGNED WITH THE DEMOCRAT PARTY

"They have a history of this. The DOJ has history of collaborating with the Democratic party interests and news media to destroy Trump. That was the purpose of Russia gate and the Mueller investigation. And 2 impeachments. FBI set people up to create negative headlines for Trump. They made the Witmer kidnapping scheme to embarrass Trump. The Jury found in April 2022 that the FBI entrapped 2 men and there was a hung jury on another 2 men. The FBI has a workspace at Perkins Coie, the leading Dem law firm in US. There is tight collaboration with the FBI and the Dems. The FBI infiltrates conservative groups. Capitol police let people in as shown on surveillance video, also the police also attacked the crowd. The police used flash bangs, rubber bullets tear gas non lethal weapons to inflame the crowd.[21]"

The FBI and the DOJ are aligned with the Democrat Party, and thus with Pelosi

The DOJ appointed a special counsel to investigate Biden and another one to investigate Trump, both in connection with the handling of classified documents. The special counsel office investigating Trump constantly leaks to the press, but the one investigating Biden never leaks to the press. Also, the prosecutor investigating Biden, Robert Hur, conducted no raids, and issued only polite requests for documents. Hur also gave the highly unusual permission for Biden's own attorneys to conduct some searches, and those lawyers may not have had security clearances. In contrast, the FBI raided Trump's home at Mar-a-Lago.

---

[21] Epoch Times video, "Jan 6, Inside Job."

The FBI has a entered into a contract with a left-wing affiliated terrorist organization associated with the Democrat Party. A group of 23 Democrat ANTIFA members attacked a police training center under construction in Georgia on March 5, 2023. One of the Antifa members arrested on domestic terrorism charges in Atlanta is a staff attorney with the Southern Poverty Law Center. The FBI has historically used the SPLC as a source for who should be considered domestic terrorists, such as the SPLC recently (January 2023) accusing many Catholics of being extremists, and then the FBI has used that false accusation in an FBI policy paper.

In 2022 Dem's fire bombed or vandalized about 80 pregnancy centers that help poor women deal with their pregnancies because the Dems view the centers as being pro-life. The Biden supporters spray painted the name of their group on the walls, 'Jane's Revenge.' Did the FBI bother to infiltrate Jane's Revenge? No. It should be easy to do. And yet the FBI arrested only three people as of January 2023. DOJ head Garland testified to Congress on March 2, 2023, 'We just couldn't find the attackers. It was night. They wore masks.' … Come on Man! You tracked down 67 year old grand-mothers from January 6 from their sweatshirt logos! And they were just taking pictures! And yet Garland has prosecuted about 30 Christians who were praying for murdered fetus's and for for their murderers outside abortion butcher centers. One guy was on a sidewalk and a male abortion employee came out and harassed the guy's 13 year old son, so the guy pushed the abortionist, defending his son as he should. No local prosecutor went after the guy, but two years later Garland and his thugs arrested him, and it only took a jury ONE hour to acquit the guy. I wonder how much the guy had to spend on lawyer's. That was probably Garland's goal.

The FBI Washington office demanded that their Boston office open up a criminal investigation of anyone who had bought a bus ticket to

DC on January 4 - 6, even if the FBI had no evidence of a crime! This violates FBI regulations and the Constitution. Boston FBI refused, despite numerous DC demands. An FBI whistleblower disclosed this to Chuck Grassley, as shown on Tucker Carlson (February 2023).

The FBI discovered who bought the Boston to DC bus tickets from Bank of America through the bank's credit card data base. The bank did not receive a subpoena but *voluntarily* gave the data to the FBI. Additionally, the bank gave the FBI other customer data relating to January 6, such as DC hotel reservations, food purchases etc. A local bank may be a better place to keep your money than at BOA, especially since BOA promotes leftist, anti-capitalist ESG investing.

*   *   *

DOJ targets a journalist they don't like

"Independent journalist Steve Baker says he was recently warned that his aggressive reporting and commentary about Jan. 6 have created growing ire at the U.S. Department of Justice that could lead to his prosecution for being at the Capitol on that fateful Wednesday in 2021.

"Since Jan. 6, Baker, 62, of Raleigh, North Carolina, went through two hours of FBI questioning and faced the looming specter of being added to the list of now more than 1,000 Jan. 6 criminal-case defendants.

"He said his recent coverage of Jan. 6 cases and pointed criticisms of the DOJ have once again painted a target on him.

"I got a call from another journalist who has a friendly source inside the Department of Justice there in D.C.," Baker told The Epoch Times.

""He called me up and said—this is a paraphrase, but he said —'Your friend in Raleigh, tell him to be careful. He has awakened a couple of people's attention to his work, and they're not happy about it at all.'"

"Baker spent much of Jan. 6 in Washington, D.C., capturing video for his news-and-commentary blog, The Pragmatic Constitutionalist. He had a front-row view of some intense scenes, including the initial bombardment of munitions aimed by police at the huge crowd on the Capitol's west front.

"His video work appeared in Jan. 6 films by HBO, The New York Times, and The Epoch Times. It has been syndicated worldwide on Storyful.

"Baker filmed the debut of a Metropolitan Police Department "hard squad" and the violence that broke out as the riot-gear-clad officers rolled and rumbled through the dense crowd like a bowling ball through a 10-pin set.

"He stood in the corner of the Capitol's south entrance as officers drew firearms near him and a group of protesters after a radio call about shots fired in the House of Representatives.

"Baker's outspokenness was on full display. He challenged two officers who drew their service weapons and shouted at unarmed protesters. The building was on high alert after reports that someone had been shot outside the Speaker's Lobby.

""Are you going to use that on us?" Baker asked one USCP officer who charged at the group. "None of us have a gun. We've got cameras."

"As the officer explained why the dozen or so law-enforcement officials in the lobby had weapons ready, Baker intoned dryly, "The only shots fired have been fired by you guys."

"Baker said if he ends up facing DOJ prosecution for being at the Capitol, it will be just the latest example of the government targeting right-of-center journalists to the exclusion of so-called mainstream media.

"Looking over a list of hundreds of Jan. 6 journalists compiled by Sedition Hunters, Baker said he could not find an example of a mainstream journalist targeted for criminal charges.

"Meanwhile, independent and right-leaning journalists such as J.D. Rivera, Sam Montoya, Stephen Horn, Will Pope, and Shawn Witzemann have faced DOJ prosecution.

""The most obvious characteristic of that list is that none of those that worked for major media, left-wing sources, have been prosecuted," Baker said. "But you can't say the same on the other side of the ledger.[22]""

*　　*　　*

FBI spies on defense lawyers

"After the close of testimony on March 22 (in a trial against The Proud Boys), prosecutors disclosed that a witness on the defense list who was due in court on March 23 had worked as an FBI informant from April 2021 until at least January 2023.

""During this period of time, the CHS ('confidential human source,' that is FBI informant) has been in contact via telephone, text messaging, and other electronic means, with one or more of the counsel for the defense and at least one defendant," the motion reads.

""The CHS also participated in prayer meetings with members of one or more of the defendants' families. The CHS also engaged in discussions with one of the defendant's family members about replacing one of the defense counsel.""[23]

*　　*　　*

An Israeli energy expert was arrested in Cypress on apparently false charges of gun smuggling in March, 2023. The judge granted him bail, but our FBI using our State Department went before the Cypress

---

[22] Joseph M Hanneman, "Journalist says DOJ targeting him for his aggressive post Jan 6 commentary," *The Epoch Times, March 30,* 2023.

[23] Joseph M Hanneman, "Defense attorney in Jan 6 case allege FBI informant spied on legal team," *The Epoch Times, March 22,* 2023.

judge and had him rescind the bail decision, keeping the man in jail. Why did the State Department do this? Because the man had reported that Hunter Biden had a mole inside the FBI named 'One-Eyed', and this mole had warned Hunter's Chinese business partners that the FBI was investigating them. The Israeli man had lived in Washington DC, and had worked with Hunter's Chinese busniness partners, and he also knew Hunter. The FBI wanted the man to be kept in prison so he could not talk to the press about Hunter's mole inside the FBI. This would be embarassing to the FBI, but also would show that the FBI is partially controlled by the Bidens and is strongly aligned with the Democrats, and thus Nancy Pelosi.[24]

FBI agent Peter Strzok "wrote emails revealing his hatred of Trump, and he said the Republican would never become president because 'We'll stop it.[25] ..."

When the FBI seized documents at Mar a Largo they spread a bunch of folders marked 'Top Secret" on the floor, took a picture, and leaked it to the press to make it look like Trump was careless. They did no such thing when they took top secret documents from Biden's garage next to the idiot's corvette. The also raided Trump's place with a subpoena, but worked out a search agreement with Biden's sleazy lawyers, agreeing not to go into certain rooms. They went into Trump's wife's panty drawers! Perverts.

After the idiot Biden let a Chinese balloon travel across the country taking photos (January 2023), the New York Times said an

---

[24] Miranda Devine, The New York Post, as she reported on Tucker Carlson, Fox News, March 23, 2023.

[25] Michael Goodwin, "Media's road to ruin in war on Trump." *The New York Post*, February 5, 2023, 12.

unnamed source from the Department of Defense stated during Trump's presidency Chinese balloons had traversed the USA, but nobody knew about it, and there were no records of it. How absurd, the DOD had no records or videos of something no one had seen, but the said it actually happened. So how do you know it happened, you liars!? Or did the venerable Times just make that up?

The FBI tried to bribe Christopher Steele, one of the architects of the Democrat's fake dossier of fake Trump Russia collusion, one million dollars to lie and say he could corroborate the dossier.[26]

The FBI lied to the FISA court to get a subpoena on Carter Page, who worked for Trump, so as to spy on Page, an American citizen. The FISA application for the subpoena stated that the FBI 'verified' the information, but the FBI did no such thing, but they sent it to the court anyway. The court found out about the lie, and did *nothing*. So much for our so called 'great' judicial system.

Biden's daughter lost her diary and the FBI eventually arrested two people in 2022 who had found it. The FBI had no right or authority to get involved with finding the diary, nor in arresting people. That is either a civil matter or for local law enforcement. Also, Ashley does not work for the government, and so the FBI should not have gotten involved. Ashley had left the diary under a mattress at a half-way house in Delray Beach, Florida. She had abandoned it. It was the property of whomever found it. It was a civil not a criminal matter for the FBI. By the way, the diary said Joe took showers with Ashley when she was a teenager.

*   *   *

---

[26] Brook Singman, Fox News, October 11, 2022.

* * *

The FBI enforcing Dem attacks on Catholics

* * *

The Democrat Party is aligned with the extreme faction of the LGBTQ leadership (not the LGBTQ rank and file), and so the fact that the FBI goes against people who oppose certain aspects of LGBTQ doctrine is further circumstantial proof of the FBI's alignment with the Dems. For example:

From The New York Post: "The FBI has now disowned its disgraceful dossier flagging multiple Catholic groups for "anti-Semitic, anti-immigrant, anti-LGBTQ and white supremacist ideology" — but only after getting publicly exposed. It's yet another sign of rank politicization, and blatant incompetence, in the nation' top law-enforcement agency.

"The central Justice Department assigned the FBI's Richmond office to draw up the target list, which then circulated nationwide. An active-duty G-man leaked it to former Special Agent Matt Seraphin, who broke the news at Uncoverdc.com.

"*Then* the Bureau killed it.

"For the record, the dossier simply flagged Catholic groups that prefer the old Latin Mass, largely superseded after Vatican II in the early '60s but still loved for its beauty and universal vision. For this, the G-men relied on the thoroughly discredited Southern Poverty Law Center, an outfit that raises big bucks by flogging lefty hysteria.

"Notably, then-Attorney General Jeff Sessions years ago ordered the entire Justice Department to stop relying on the SPLC after it got caught slandering Muslim reformers and mislabeling religious-freedom groups. Did Attorney General Merrick Garland quietly rescind that order?

"After all, this follows Garland's highly political noise about sticking the FBI on parents who speak up at school-board meetings, not to mention the Bureau's politicized bumbling in the Russiagate investigation, turning bogus opposition research commissioned by the Hillary Clinton campaign into a phony scandal that (with disgraceful media collusion) plagued the Trump administration for years.

"Don't forget its utter botching of the Hillary Clinton email "probe," which somehow ignored the former secretary of state's years-long, illegal retention of classified info *and* willful destruction of evidence.

"Bad enough that this anti-Catholic farce diverted resources from the work the FBI *should* be doing, suggesting that its entire anti-domestic-terror effort is a complete fraud. Far worse is that it shows the Bureau (at least, the high command in DC) hasn't remotely mended its ways after all those embarrassments.[27]"

"The FBI fabricated a non-existent group they called "radical-traditionalist Catholics", that they characterized as having "frequent adherence to anti-semetic, anti-immigrant, anti-LGBTQ, and white supremacist ideology." The FBI cited the left-wing Southern Poverty Law Center as well as "FBI investigations, local law enforcement agency reporting, and liason reporting, with varying degrees of corroboration and access." After being exposed by a whistleblower The FBI disavowed the report as it did not meet the "exacting standards of the FBI.[28]"

What a joke from a bunch of incompetent fools! The FBI author should be fired, lose his pension and lose his health care. Wray is an incompetent idiot. The Southern Poverty Law Center is a left-wing terrorist organization. Has the FBI reviewed the Center's finances that the Center keeps off shore? Are they funded by Putin or some billionaire extreme left-winger who both want to destroy the USA? Is the FBI corroborating with a Putin financed organization?

*   *   *

---

[27] Editorial, "Proof the FBI's Still Broken," *The New York Post*, Feb 18, 2023, 24.

[28] Samantha Flom, "State AGs seek answers fromFBI, DOJ over targeting of Catholics," *The Epoch Times*, Feb 15 - 21, 2023, 1,

* * *

Matt Gaetz is an aggressive conservative Republican who the Dems despise because of his strong attacks against Democrats. So the Dems silenced him for two years by having the Department of Justice, which is affiliated politically and actually with the FBI. Someone at the DOJ 'leaked' a lie that Matt was being investigated for sex trafficking of teenage girls. (how do you leak something that is not true? Well they did it at the DOJ. Surprise, surprise) The New York Times reported this lie, and cited 'unnamed sources.' Yea, right. This shut a loud Republican down for two years. Even Fox News would not have him own for fear of embarrassment if the lie was true. So much for innocent until proven guilty at Fox News Liberals would hold up posters that said 'Rapist' when Matt held press conferences. Then miraculously in February 2023 the DOJ announced he was not being investigated. The DOJ knew that two years earlier. It was not a complicated thing to investigate — just interview one woman. The DOJ/FBI had purposely said nothing so as to shut an outspoken Republican down during the midterm election cycle. Just like what they do in a Banana Republic. Garland and Wray are ruining this country.

* * *

The FBI has a personal workstation in the Washington office of Perkins Coie, a law firm with deep ties to the Democratic Party and a string of Democratic presidential campaigns, The Washington Times has learned. (June 2022)

Democrat lawyer Michael Sussman had an FBI badge that got him into the FBI building.

FBI agent threatens repairman: "…nothing happens to people that don't talk …"

"The computer repair shop owner who blew the whistle on Hunter Biden's infamous laptop claims in a new book that an FBI agent threatened him to stay silent.

"John Paul Mac Isaac said two federal agents came to his Mac Shop in Wilmington, Del. in December 2019 to recoup the laptop following a subpoena, he details in his new book "American Injustice: My Battle to Expose the Truth."

"The repairman, who had volunteered to hand the laptop over to the feds two months earlier, said the alleged threat came after he made a joke, telling them: "Hey, lads, I'll remember to change your names when I write the book."

""Agent Wilson kept walking but Agent DeMeo paused and turned to face me," Paul Mac writes of the encounter.

"Isaac said the agent then told him: "It is our experience that nothing ever happens to people that don't talk about these things."

"The owner said he locked the door after the agents walked out, leaving him to "digest the encounter."

""Was I being paranoid, or had what the agent just told me been a direct threat, or at best a thinly veiled one?" he writes." New York Post, August 12, 2022.

*　*　*　*　*

The judge gave $ to Obama

The judge who signed the FBI search warrant for the seizure of documents at Mar-a-Largo had contributed thousands to Obama's campaigns. July 2022.

The slimy FBI in-house lawyer

An FBI lawyer, Clinesmith, altered evidence and submitted it to a court resulting in nearly ruining Carter Paige's life. Clinesmith pleaded guilty, and received a minor penalty. The FBI did not care that they employed a dirtball (in fact, they probably asked him to alter the evidence). They continued his employment, and the DC Bar Association did not revoke his license. Other people at the FBI would have known about the crime and participated in it, but they were not charged. Clinesmith got his job back at the FBI and was not disbarred (unlike the Missouri lawyer McCloskey who was disbarred for protecting his home and wife from a mob. He never fired his gun) … The Bar Association is corrupt and run by Dem ambulance chasers. …

FBI offers a $1 million bribe to a guy to get him to corroborate a FBI lie

The FBI offered a former British intelligence officer $1 million to corroborate the fake Russian dossier, paid for by the Clinton campaign, that the FBI knew at the time was false. Newsmax, Oct 12, 2022, 'Republicans Blast …' by Solange Reyner.

FBI not following their own regulations (re Hunter)

An FBI whistleblower has reported that the FBI shut down the investigation into Hunter's laptop without giving a reason, as required by FBI regulations. Fox News, Tucker Carlson, July 27, 2022.

'You're innocent? So what? What does that have to do with anything?'

In June 2022, 19 months after the Jan 6 protest, the FBI arrested the Republican front runner for Michigan governor (Ryan Kelley) on 4 misdemeanor charges. Why did the FBI wait? To help the Mich Dems? He has denied ever being in the building. If he was arrested for encouraging people to enter, why has Ray Epps not been arrested. Epps is clearly on tape inciting crimes.

* * *

'Peter Navarro, put him in leg irons'

The FBI are criminals. They followed Trump's economic adviser Peter Navarro to the DC airport and put him in leg irons and handcuffs and then threw him in solitary. For what? He legally challenged an illegal Congressional subpoena from the illegally constituted Jan 6 Committee. He was not at the Capitol on Jan 6, and the FBI knows that. He lives 2 blocks from FBI headquarters. He has never been arrested. The charge is white collar, not criminal. There was no flight risk. … The FBI never arrested Eric Holder for challenging a Congressional subpoena when he sent weapons of war to drug lords in Mexico. … I guess poor Peter is just in the wrong party. We live in a banana republic thanks to Christopher Wray, the asshole, and Garland, the fascist. June 2022.

FBI cover up

"Newly released notes taken by high-level Department of Justice officials at a March 6, 2017 meeting with FBI leadership expose some of the lengths the FBI went to, to cover up their corruption and malfeasance in spying on President Donald Trump.

"The notes were released earlier this week by lawyers for Hillary Clinton's campaign lawyer Michael Sussmann as part of an effort to clear Sussmann for having lied to the FBI. In reality, while the notes do little to exonerate Sussmann, they provide quite a bit to incriminate the FBI.

"The meeting at which the notes were taken took place just two days after Trump's infamous March 4, 2017 tweet in which he accused former President Obama of having wiretapped Trump Tower. Trump's tweet panicked FBI leadership, who were unsure exactly how much Trump knew about their efforts to set him up. In response to Trump's tweet, they tried to cover their tracks with another layer of lies and deception.

"The FBI leadership told a series of lies to acting attorney general

Boente about their Trump investigation. The FBI reports to the DOJ."
The Epoch Times, May 11, 2022, 'New DOJ Notes From 2017 Reveal
FBI Panic After Trump Tweeted That He Knew He Was Being Spied On
| Truth Over News', by Jeff Carlson and Han Mahmcke.

FBI Leftists conduct a purge of Trump supporters

The FBI is purging some Trump supporters from its staff. Even
though FBI employees had the first amendment right to go to Trump's
rally, if you were there, the FBI strips you of your security clearance.
Which means you can't work for the FBI. The Epoch Times, May 7,
2022.

Different DOJ standards for Libs and Conservatives

"As deputy director of the FBI, and later as acting director,
McCabe demonstrated his contempt for constitutional legal principles
—such as the Fifth Amendment protection against self-incrimination
and the Sixth Amendment right to effective counsel—considered as
essential cornerstones to a free society by the framers and enshrined
in Bill of Rights, when, as reported by Greg Re for Fox News, Andrew
McCabe counseled Lt. Gen. Michael Flynn to forgo the presence of an
attorney during a hostile interrogation masquerading as an amicable
interview.

"Instead, an investigation by the Department of Justice Office of
the Inspector General, released in February 2018, found several
instances of "lack of candor" by McCabe while providing sworn
testimony. Subsequently, Inspector General Michael Horowitz referred
the matter to the U.S. attorney in Washington for criminal
prosecution.

"The order to fire McCabe didn't arise from a political source, nor
did it come from the Trump White House. Rather, it came from the
FBI's Office of Professional Responsibly (OPR), the bureau's version of
Internal Affairs.

"Concurrent with a no-doubt lucrative run as a CNN commentator, McCabe has been formally absolved of wrongdoing by a Garland Department of Justice (DOJ) settlement.

"McCabe's pension has been fully restored, and all references to his having been fired for cause are to be removed from official FBI files. Also, a strong message was sent to special counsel John Durham that in today's DOJ, his criminal referrals of high-profile anti-Trump players may be destined for the dustbin of politicized justice.

"Adding insult to injury, more than $500,000 in legal fees will be paid by the DOJ to McCabe's attorneys, the white-shoe law firm of Arnold and Porter.

"And virtually unreported by media outlets was the DOJ's settlement with Trump national security adviser John Bolton.

"In sharp contradistinction to the McCabe settlement are the recent FBI executed search warrants on Project Veritas Director James O'Keefe and several of his journalists, demonstrating, in no uncertain terms, that the truth doesn't pay.

"The purported justification for the government action appears to arise from a diary maintained by (and subsequently lost by) Ashley Biden, daughter of President Joe Biden. Compounding the government's seemingly tenuous justification for search and seizure in a constitutionally protected domain—that of the First Amendment —are leaks to The New York Times, as reported by Andrew McCarthy on Nov. 12 in The National Review —apparently calculated to cast the organization in a negative light.

"The McCabe settlement rewrote history, virtually erasing from official records the acts that prompted a criminal referral by the Department of Justice's own inspector general. It remains to be seen whether taxpayer dollars will also be used to defray O'Keefe's legal expenses." The Epoch Times, December 21, 2021, 'Department of Justice Has Different Standards for Different Subjects,' by Marc Ruskin.

FBI malfeasance and incompetence

The New York Post listed FBI malfeasance and incompetence (New York Post, Nov 19, 2021, "How the FBI Went Bad" by Victor Davis Hanson):

"Investigating and tracking parents who confront school boards.

FBI head Lying Jimmy Comey allowed H Clinton's private computer contractor, CrowdStrike, to run the investigation of the hack and keep possession of hard drives associated with it.

During Robert Mueller's special investigation the FBI "implausibly claimed it had no idea how requested information on cell phones mysteriously disappeared."

Under Comey the FBI submitted lies in requests for warrants to the FISA court.

FBI lawyer Kevin Clinesman forged elements of an affidavit to surveil Trump aid Carter Page. Good old Kevin boy changed it from "Page worked for the CIA" to Page DID NOT work for the CIA. A 100 percent change. I believe Kevin still works for the FBI (why?). He pleaded guilty.

The FBI hired lying and disreputable ex-British spy Christopher Steele as a contractor while he was peddling fantasies.

"Former FBI General Counsel James Baker was reportedly the subject of a federal investigation for meetings with media outlets that later leaked lurid tales from the Steele dossier. He also met repeatedly with now indicted Perkins Coe attorney Michael Sussman."

Comey admitted he leaked his confidential memos detailing his private meetings with President Trump.

"In sworn testimony to Congress Comey on 245 occasions claimed he could not remember or had no knowledge of key elements of his own 'Russian Collusion' investigation."

FBI Comey replacement Andrew 'The Dick' McCabe was fired for leaking sensitive information to the so called 'Media. He lied on at least 3 occasions to federal attorneys and his own FBI investigators. Now on CNN he offers misleading information on the Russian hoax he helped promulgate.

Mueller testified to Congress that he 'claimed' he had little or no knowledge about Fusion GI's or the Steele Dossier – the sources that birthed the entire collusion hoax. … What a LIAR … or a doddering old alzheimer infected idiot … or a guy who acts like an alzheimer idiot, but is really a flim-flam man who is pretending to be a fool so he and his family can scam us all, and make tons of money

The FBI sent a huge swat team to Ft Lauderdale to arrest a 70 year old man with no criminal record, and with no reason to believe he was violent. Oh, they were afraid of his 70 year old wife? They even had a gun boat in the canal behind the house. The man was Roger Stone, of course. … Wimps. … Oh, and they contacted CNN first so the douche bags could be on the scene to film the morons (the FBI agents that is).

The FBI stormed the house of Project Veritas head James O'Keefe to do the personal work of Joe Biden, getting his daughter's diary back. … This action of Biden's is the crime of 'stealing government' resources" since the FBI work was for personal benefits, such as using city public works people to install a hot tub at your house while they are on city worktime.

The FBI did not disclose that it possessed Hunter B's laptop, while the main stream media declared the NY Post reporting on was Russian disinformation.

US Olympic doctor Lasser Nassar was a known and chronic child molester. The perverts at the FBI downed-played the evidence. Several gymnasts have sued the FBI over this.

12 FBI agents or informants had leadership roles in the in the kidnapping scheme of Michigan governor Gretchen Whitmer."

*   *   *

FBI stated they only track right wing 'violent' groups, and not left wing 'violent' groups. Left wing groups caused 527 violent riots in

2020. Oct. 3, 2021.

The FBI threw a man in prison for a month simply for going into the Capitol Building for 50 *seconds* on January 6. The prosecutor stated that the man, Daniel Goodwyn, neither attacked nor threatened anyone, nor harmed any property. There is building security footage showing the man entering and then immediately exiting the building. The DOJ then put him under house arrest for *one year*. He now faces possibly one year in prison. This is political persecution, banana republic, Vladimir Putin, Joseph Stalin, Joe Biden, Christopher Wray, Merrick Garland style.[29]

McCabe: FBI criminal lies, keeps his pension, and gets a gig on CNN

FBI liar Andrew McCabe got his pension back and a lot of legal fees, per an order from Biden's DOJ. Sessions under Trump fired him. The DOJ Inspector General report called him a 'serial liar', gave details and recommended he be fired for lack of candor. He also signed the bogus and politically motivated FISA warrant used to illegally spy on Trump campaign advisor Carter Page. He lied multiple times while under oath to the IG and to FBI investigators. He improperly leaked sensitive info to the Wall Street Journal and then lied about it to FBI director James Comey. Katie Pavlich of Town Hall, October 15, 2021. …. Why did Barr not prosecute him? Roger Stone and General Flynn were prosecuted for much smaller transgressions. How about the two 67 year old ladies who were prosecuted for walking around the Capital Building for 15 minutes and causing no violence nor property damage on Jan 6? Huh

'You're a conservative journalist? Well, you're screwed.' Project Veritas

---

[29] Tucker Carlson Show, March 14, 2023.

* * *

The FBI raided journalist Project Veritas home to get Biden's daughter's journal even though the Project Veritas had not stolen the diary, and they had bought it. Project Veritas had given the journal to the police many months earlier. Project Veritas decided not to publish it. The FBI also took the president of Project Veritas's phone, with donor names etc. Seven agents were in the raid, and they handcuffed him. This is unprecedented. The diary was not government property, and Project Veritas did not steal it … The FBI had no business dealing with the diary. Third world, banana republic stuff. … The New York Times had got Trump's tax returns, illegally stolen. Did the FBI raid the NYT? No way! Nov 8, 2021.

FBI Kavanaugh tip line

Per an FBI letter to the Senate: Justice Kavanaugh's nomination "was the first time that the FBI set-up a tip line for a nominee undergoing Senate confirmation," and that tip line received "over 4,500 tips. Source: Senator (RI) Whitehouse's website. July 2022.

FBI spies on Trump

The FBI spied on the Trump Campaign in 2016, using the fake Steel dossier as a pretext, knowing the dossier was all lies and fabrications.

Comey screws his boss

Comey met with Trump about the Steel dossier even though Comey knew it was a total fabrication. He did the meeting because doing so allowed him to release the fake dossier to the press.

'Ha ha ha, we got them.' Comey

Comey said in an interview that he knew he was breaking White House protocol by sending 2 agents to interview General Flynn without first clearing the meeting with White House counsel. Comey laughed about it while speaking at a conference, and bragged. A crime??

Two systems of justices. Barr, why did you fail to prosecute?

"One of Justice Brett M. Kavanaugh's accusers admitted this week that she made up her lurid tale of a backseat car rape, saying it "was a tactic" to try to derail the judge's confirmation to the Supreme Court. Sen. Chuck Grassley, chairman of the Judiciary Committee revealed the fraud in a letter to the FBI and Justice Department Friday, asking them to prosecute Judy Munro-Leighton for lying to and obstructing Congress. Mr. Grassley's investigators tried to reach her for a month but were unsuccessful until this week, when they spoke to her by phone and she confessed that she was not the original Jane Doe, and "did that as a way to grab attention." The FBI did nothing. Associated Press , Nov 3, 2018, 'Kavanaugh accuser admits to making up rape allegation ...' by Stephan Dinan.

Agents erase texts

Two FBI agents connected to the FBI's involvement with the Russian hoax erased the texts on their cell phones. They worked for special prosecutor Mueller. He did nothing to them. This is a crime. 'Obstruction of Justice.' 2018.

WHY no prosecution, Barr? False Kavanaugh accuser, Rhode Island boat rape claim

"A Rhode Island man who claimed U.S. Supreme Court nominee Brett Kavanaugh sexually assaulted a woman aboard a boat in Rhode Island more than 30 years ago apologized Wednesday, saying he "made a mistake." The FBI did nothing.

* * *

Strzok to his FBI lover, "It's an insurance policy"

FBI lawyer Lisa Paige asked her FBI lover Peter Strzok, 'Trump will never become president, will he?' Strzok said, 'No. No he's not. *We'll* stop it.' Later he said, 'It's like an insurance policy' we have against him becoming president. Strzok never faced legal consequences.

Lock her up!

FBI head James Comey said Hillary Clint's actions regarding her emails and server were criminal conduct, but she did not 'have an intent to commit a crime.' He said, 'No reasonable prosecutor would bring charges.' As a result, he said what she did was not a crime! … Plus, it was not Comey's decision to make. It was the AG's, Lynch. And Lynch then could have still prosecuted Clinton, but instead she just relied on Comey so that Lynch was not put in a position of having to clear Clinton. …. Compare this to what the FBI did to General Flynn. The field agents said that Flynn did not lie to them, and the case was being closed until the criminal McCabe reopened it, and prosecuted Flynn. 2016.

The secret service hides Hunter's gun purchase fraudulent records

The secret service improperly confiscated Hunter's gun purchase records from the the seller, which showed he had lied to get the gun by saying he did not take drugs. The secret service is not supposed to act as a private citizen's baby sitter.

FBI brass illegally uses their cell phones to take photos of the Mar-a-Lago documents

The FBI has stored the documents seized from Mar-a-Lago in an

FBI secured facility at their their headquarters, where no one is allowed to take FBI or personal cell phones. The FBI tech department noted multiple cell phone transmissions from the facility. It turns out that FBI senior brass were taking phones into the facility, taking pictures of sensitive documents, and sending them to the Washington Post. FBI whistleblowers told this to the Washington Times. FBI leaders shut down their own tech department from monitoring this, and they are doing their own 'internal investigation'. Ha Ha, that's a joke. Jesse Watters, Sept 12, 2022.

FBI suppresses Tony Bobulinski

The FBI had plenty of evidence from Tony Bobulinski, one of Hunter Biden's business partners, showing that Joe profited personally by using US foreign aid as a tool to enable Joe's business partner and son, Hunter, make millions of dollars. An FBI agent Timothy Thibault, hid and suppressed this information. The FBI interviewed Bobulinski 11 days before the 2020 election, and then hid the interview. Tony met with Joe the Fool twice. Tony gave the FBI 2 cell phones showing texts with Hunter, and they have disappeared. ... There is a grand jury in Delaware investigating Hunter, the sex addict, but they have *never* interviewed Bobulinski. Aug 30, 2022.

The Laptop - more stuff

FBI whistleblowers have told Sen Grassley that they had possession of the laptop in their field office, but FBI brass told them not to look at it until after the election. Fox News, Aug 25, 2022.

FBI censors laptop reporting at Facebook

Facebook's Zuckerberg said that the FBI told him 2 weeks before the 2020 election to censor the Hunter Biden laptop story. On a Joe Rogan podcast Zuckerberg said: "The FBI, I think, basically came to us - some folks on our team - and was like, 'Hey, just so you know, like, you should be on high alert… We thought that there was a lot of Russian propaganda in the 2016 election. We have it on notice that, basically, there's about to be some kind of dump of that's similar to that. So just be vigilant.'"

The FBI issued a statement to media outlets on Friday, saying that its warning to Facebook was of a general nature and did not include a call to action.

Zuckerberg told Rogan as much on the podcast when asked whether the FBI specified that Facebook needed to "be on guard" about the **Hunter Biden** laptop story.

"No. I don't remember if it was that specifically. But it was, it basically fit the pattern," Zuckerberg replied.

The FBI said it "routinely notifies U.S. private sector entities, including social media providers, of potential threat information, so that they can decide how to better defend against threats" and that the agency "has provided companies with foreign threat indicators to help them protect their platforms and customers from abuse by foreign malign influence actors."

….. OK FBI if that is true: why did you go to Facebook right before the laptop article came out in the New York Post? How often had you sent agents in person to Facebook in the past? What other Russian disinformation were you worried about at that time that would have caused you to send agents to Facebook? …. Why are you such lying assholes? Do you realize you have interfered with US election 1000 times more than the Russians have? August 26, 2022.

Suppression of Hunter's laptop by the FBI and Big Tech "changed the course of history"

Miranda Devine of the New York Post commented, "We know from polls taken by the Media Research Center straight after the election that there was something like one in six Biden voters would have changed their vote if they had known about this story. And in an election that was won by, I think, 45,000 votes in a handful of battleground states, that would have made a material difference. So Facebook, Twitter, the FBI interfered in the election and they changed the course of history. And for Mark Zuckerberg to sit there with Joe Rogan and Joe Rogan to kind of happily accept what he's saying with very little pushback is kind of sickening." Fox News, Aug 26, 2022.

Hillary illegally deleted email

Hillary Clinton deleted 33,000 emails after she received a subpoena, which is a criminal act, and then lapdog Comey of the FBI would not prosecute her. His lame excuse: "No reasonable prosecutor would prosecute her for that." Will unreasonable prosecutors prosecuted Republicans for much less. Hillary's staff also destroyed cell phone sim cards with hammers.

Comey's wife and four daughters were all huge H. Clinton fans, as shown on photos of them at H. Clinton rallies. Comey is unlikely to have political views different from the people he loves.

THE ADMINISTRATIVE STATE IS ALLIGNED WITH THE DEMOCRATS

Pelosi and the Dems control the administrative state including, the FBI, the CIA and the rest of the intelligence community. And the CIA most likely had agents in the Trump crowd posing as supporters. These agents likely initiated some of the violence. The CIA specializes in causing ferment in foreign countries, and they easily can import their methods to the US. The people in DC largely work for the government, that is the administrative state, and they voted 95 percent for Biden. The Dems thus control the administrative state. This is further circumstantial efforts that a jury could consider in determining Pelosi's guilt or innocence.

Below are a few events that show how the CIA etc went after Trump, thus providing evidence that given that the CIA likely had agents on January 6 in the Trump crowd causing violence, this was done at the behest of Pelosi.

In Trump's first week in office, the CIA released a transcript of Trump's first call with a foreign leader, a confidential call. Nothing controversial or significant was in the call. They did this to intimidate Trump. The CIA is scum, and works against our democracy. They said Iraq had weapons of mass destruction, when Iraq did not, causing us to invade and occupy it for years, causing massive deaths and destruction, and the complete annihilation of the large Iraq Christian community.

Alexander Vindman, a deep state operator on Trump's National Security Council, illegally leaked a phone Trump had with the Ukraine president. He broke the chain of command and should have been court marshalled. His boss determined that the call was proper, as did the Senate during the clown-show impeachment. There was no quid pro quo nor delay in the shipment of weapons to Ukraine. Just because Biden was a political rival does not mean he should not be investigated for possible crimes of using foreign aid to enrich himself through his son. If Biden had raped a Ukrainian woman working in the US embassy, would it have been improper for Trump to ask the Ukrainians to investigate that even if Biden was a political rival? Lunacy. That is what the Dems and Romney would say. What plane are those fools from?

Trump visited a giant World War II cemetery in Normandy, France to attend a ceremony marking the 75th anniversary of D Day. The press said that an 'unnamed source' said Trump called the dead soldiers 'suckers.' Another lie from the press or from the deep state. To make such a ridiculous claim the press needs some type of corroboration. Also, the term 'poor suckers' is an expression that conveys sympathy towards the people you are referring to. It means you feel sorry for someone who was unjustly harmed. It's a term that was commonly used by Americans born before 1955. So most CIA employees are younger and not familiar with the term, and are also culturally illiterate. After all, they likely went to Ivy League schools. They would also lie given their hatred for Trump, and have heard Trump say 'poor suckers' but pass it on to the press as 'suckers.'

After the USA defeated ISIS in Syria, Trump ordered all US forces out of Syria. Did our military obey this order by our constitution's commander and chief? Trump's Secretary of Defense, Mark Esper, disobeyed the order, and kept troops in Syria, and hid that fact from Trump. Esper admitted this in his book and on TV news. So Esper believes in neither the chain of command nor our constitution nor democracy. He believes the president, elected by the people, can be overruled by a bureaucrat. He believes he is wiser than the elected president, and so he can do whatever he wants. I would trust Trump's judgment over Esper's. Additionally, Esper has a conflict of interest in that he wants wars to go on. He will be employed or sit on boards of defense contractors who earn more money when the wars go on and on.

* * *

The ex-acting head of the CIA, John McLaughlin, admitted that the Deep State exists when he said on a TV show, "Thank god the the Deep State, They have kept Trump in check.[30]" ... Obviously, this wanker doesn't believe that duly elected people should run the government in a democracy. God help us from fools like John McLaughlin.

---

[30] Fox News, January 11, 2019.

RAY EPPS

Video from January 6 clearly shows Ray Epps setting up Trump supporters by demanding that they go into The Capitol Building and then be falsely charged with trespass or some absurd crime. So he was clearly a weapon for the Democrat party. And yet even though the FBI saw the videos and he admitted to the FBI the videos were accurate, the FBI never arrested him. So Epps was aligned with the Democrat party, the FBI should have arrested him and did not, and thus this is further circumstantial evidence that the FBI is aligned with the Democrats.

Below is a summary of Epp's January 6 story.

RAY EPPS — THE SUMMARY

Ray Epps is a large, loud man, and was seen in several videos urging people to go *into* theCapitol building. Also, Epps told the FBI per FBI transcripts that he **told Jan 6 protesters to break INTO the Capitol building.** And yet, amazingly, *HE HAS NEVER BEEN ARRESTED!!*

Ray Epps broke the law by telling people to break into the Capitol building. He and the FBI both acknowledge this. The FBI never arrested him.

Prosecutors have prosecuted *ANYONE AND EVERYONE* who even remotely was connected to the protest. Even if they never went into the building. For example, they prosecuted two 67 year old grandmothers who were waived into the building by the police, who threatened no one, who caused no property damage, and who were in the building for only 15 minutes. They prosecuted a DEA agent (who was on his own time) who didn't even go into the building. His crime? 'Standing on a national monument.' He had stood on the base of a column outside the building!

The January 6 Committee released a text from Epps to his son where he said, "I was in the front with a few others. I orchestrated it."

The FBI never arrested Epps. They knew where he lived. They had Epps on their 10 most wanted list for a few weeks, and then took him off, without giving an explanation.

FBI head Wray testified under oath that the FBI has undercover agents at all major rallies, and had them at Jan 6. FBI agents who commit crimes while acting as informants, when done in the course of their duties, are never prosecuted. They are call 'unindicted co-conspirators.' They are common.

Epps has said he did not work for the FBI nor any other government agency.

So the million dollar question is: *WHY DID THE FBI NEVER ARREST RAY EPPS? THEY HAVE ARRESTED EVERYBODY ELSE.* All the evidence shows he committed a crime(s) by telling people to break into the Capitol building.

The US government is a propaganda machine here in the USA and abroad

Emily Grace Rainey was a captain with the Psychological Operations Group at Fort Bragg, NC. She said she essentially was a propagandist. She noted the term 'terrorist' is purposely kept vague so as to capture as many people as possible. The Dept. of Homeland Security posted 'Potential Terror Threats include: Opposition to COVID measures … claims of election fraud … 9/11 anniversary and religious holidays.' February 2021. … She led a group of friends to Trump's Jan 6 rally. She never went in. The FBI lied, and said she went there with 'weapons and military equipment.' Fort Bragg ruined her career – they revoked her clearance, denied her a commission in the reserves, and they put a gag order on her until October 2021, so she could not tell the public what they need to hear.

Since its inception the CIA has used propaganda to influence the populations of countries around the world, from Russia to Nicaragua. It is well documented that the CIA is aligned with the Democratic party, and they dislike Trump and his supporters. Every CIA ex-official who speaks on the TV news identifies themselves as a Democrat. The CIA recruits heavily from Ivy League schools. Over 80% of the graduates from those schools are Democrats. In Trump's first week in office the CIA illegally leaked a transcript of one of Trump first phone calls with a foreign leader.

The head of the FBI, Christopher Wray, stated that the FBI always has undercover agents at events like the Jan 6 Election Justice Protest. The CIA also does. And both would be doing what they could to make Trump and his supporters look bad using their propaganda machines.

RAY EPPS — THE DETAILS (in reverse chronological order)

Epps thought there was going to be a bombing (Reported Aug 24, 2022)

From The Epoch Times: "The Epoch Times has obtained from the FBI a collection of Epps-related material obtained by the newspaper, including FBI interview summaries, FBI audio recordings, transcripts, videos, and photographs.

Records obtained by The Epoch Times show that Epps Sr. believed there would be a bomb attack on a side street of Washington on Jan. 6, 2021, which prompted him to bring a first-aid kit when he traveled to the city from Arizona.

Epps Sr. told FBI agents in March 2021 that he only came to Washington on Jan. 6, 2021, because he wanted to look after his son, who decided to make the trip from his home in Utah with a friend.

FBI agents didn't press Epps Sr. or his son for more details on the bomb fears. Nor did they ask about the two alleged pipe bombs found outside the Republican and Democratic party headquarters, each just blocks from the Capitol. Why didn't the FBI press Epps for more details? Because the FBI thought he worked for the CIA or another such agency?

Videos from the night of Jan. 5, 2021, show Epps Sr. engaging in discussions with Trump supporters and urging them to go into the Capitol the next day.

Epps Sr. shouted to the crowd: "Tomorrow, we need to go into the Capitol. Into the Capitol. Peacefully."

The crowd then started chanting, "Fed! Fed! Fed! Fed!"

Video evidence from the west side backs up stories the men told about Epps Sr. trying to deescalate problems when protesters became instigators at the police line. Several times, he confronted agitators and told them to back off or step back from the police line.

A Metropolitan Police Department bodycam captured Epps Sr. chiding one man who was shouting at police.

"They're not the enemy," he said. About a minute later, he physically restrained a young man and told him, "Nobody needs to get hurt. Back off, man, just stop."

Other actions caught on video continue to generate questions, however. At one point, the crowd started passing a giant fabric billboard in a metal frame. *The billboard was eventually rammed into the police line.* Some protesters who handled the sign are being charged with assault on police.

One video reviewed by The Epoch Times shows Epps Sr. with a hand on the sign helping to pass it along.

Eric Clark of northern Kentucky, who stood next to Epps Sr. at the police line on the west side, said Epps Sr. made a strange statement after learning that Clark had been in the U.S. Marine Corps.

"He says, 'Semper Fidelis, devil dog, we got to hold this crowd back a little longer, or they're gonna [expletive] up the plan,'" Clark told The Epoch Times. "Okay, there's some kind of plan?"

Clark also said he saw Epps Sr. pull a man out of the crowd, and the man and two associates went up along a wall near a staircase and pulled the lid off a utility hatch.

The men removed a long two-by-four piece of lumber; a long, heavy-duty cardboard tube; and a small ladder.

The two-by-four and the cardboard tube were later passed through the crowd outside the Lower West Terrace tunnel.

The tube was used as a battering ram to smash a window adjacent to the tunnel, video shows.

Through his attorney, Epps Sr. denied Clark's story. The Epoch Times, Aug 24, 2022, 'Epps showed son how to use a tourniquet ....', by Joseph Hanneman.

New FBI material on Epps (Reported Aug 19, 2022)

The Epoch Times just got a collection of Ray Epps related material from the FBI, including interview summaries, videos, transcripts etc. Epps admitted that he was guilty of trespassing on restricted Capitol grounds and confessed to urging protesters to go to – and into – the Capitol on Jan 6, 2021.

Despite these admissions the FBI never arrested him, and the DOJ never prosecuted him.

The DOJ just convicted a 67 year old woman with cancer to 3 months in federal prison for entering into the Capitol after the police waved her in. She was in the building for 15 minutes and took tourist pictures, harmed no one, threatened no one, and destroyed no property.

(I guess the DOJ likes large, violent men but not frail older ladies.)

He has been caught on video doing things that he failed to mention to the FBI when he called the FBI on Jan 8: On Jan 5 he urged the crowds to go into the Capitol the next day (he said he was in the crowd to calm things down). Also he is on video on Jan 6 on a bullhorn at the Trump rally far from the Capitol encouraging people to go to the Capitol. He mentioned these acts 2 months later to the FBI.

He told the FBI he received 5 ballots at his Queens Creek address, 3 of which were for people who didn't live there.

Epps told the Jan 6 fake committee that he was not working for any law enforcement agency on Jan 5 and 6. He said he was a Trump supporter and thought there had been election fraud.

At hearings when Sen Ted Cruz asked FBI top officials about Epps, they said repeatedly, "I can't answer that."

Why can't they answer? Why wasn't he arrested? Why did Kinzinger call Epps a 'hero? Why won't the Jan 6 fake committee release the full transcript of Epps' testimony? Aug 19, 2022.

More Ray Epps videos (Reported July 2022)

Newly released video shows Ray Epps standing on a street corner in DC telling people they should march to the Capitol, and giving directions by pointing to where to go for the Capitol. July 2022.

* * *

Eric Clark (Reported June 28, 2022)

From the Epoch Times: " Ray Epps, the former Arizona Oath Keepers leader who was famously captured on camera a day before the Jan. 6, 2021, protests urging people to go into the U.S. Capitol, allegedly directed a group of individuals who removed "siege weapons," including a long piece of 2-by-4-inch lumber, from a utility hatch on Capitol grounds after telling a witness they needed to slow the crowd so it didn't "[expletive] up the plan," a Kentucky man claims.

Eric Clark, 45, says he encountered Epps on the west side of the Capitol on Jan. 6, 2021, although he didn't realize who he was until he saw news reports about Epps earlier this year. He said that behavior and statements he witnessed took on new meaning after he read news reports about Epps's possible role as a provocateur at the Capitol.

"I didn't know who Ray Epps was," Clark told The Epoch Times. "I just knew a tall mountain of a man who said something to me, and I saw some things occur.

Epps has long denied being an informant for the FBI or other law enforcement entity on Jan. 6. His photo—assigned No. 16—was initially placed on the FBI's Jan. 6 most-wanted website, but it was later removed without explanation. Epps hasn't been arrested or charged with crimes for being at the Capitol.

Clark said Epps then pulled a man from the crowd.

"Mr. Epps had already come back down to our end, he grabbed a man in a black hoodie out of the crowd," Clark said. "He said something to him and he marches off to the right, where all the Capitol guards were."

What happened next is still burned in Clark's memory.

"The other gentleman pulled out [by Epps] in the black hoodie pulls two other people out of the crowd, and they make a beeline directly toward this structure," Clark said. "It's like 4 foot by 4 foot by 4 foot, and it has a hatch like a lid on top of it."

The men pulled the hatch, and from inside this utility access retrieved a 12-foot-long piece of 2-by-4-inch lumber, a piece of thick cardboard tubing of about the same length, and a stepstool approximately 3 feet tall, he said. The cardboard tube was about 6 inches in diameter.

Epps moved away from the group after speaking to the first man and didn't help the men remove the alleged siege tools, Clark said.

"I looked down in it [the structure] and it appears to be like utility or wet-wall access, some type of drain clean-out or whatever, but it's definitely some type of small tunnel area," he said, "where they're pulling all this stuff out of."

Clark said one of the men wore a bright red or orange hat. One of the other men wore a tan Carhartt-style jacket.

One of the items Clark said he witnessed being pulled from the utility hatch matches a video of an unidentified man vandalizing a window at the Capitol. The man, known only by the hashtag #RedOnRedGlasses, has not been identified or charged, although the FBI lists him as No. 300 on its Jan. 6 most-wanted page.

John Blischak, Epps's Phoenix-based attorney, denied Clark's assertions.

"I have read your comments and as Mr. Epps stated: 'It never happened,'" Blischak told The Epoch Times in an email. "I do not question his integrity whatsoever."

Videos from the day show items similar to those described by Clark being passed around as weapons at the entrance to the Lower West Terrace tunnel. A short stepladder was also seen inside the tunnel entrance. It isn't known where those items came from.

Video shows Epps in several places on the Capitol grounds chiding protesters for violence and urging them to let police officers do their jobs without interference. One man seemed to be threatening the police line on the west side of the Capitol when Epps intervened.

"I'd love to [expletive] get it on," the man said. "I would have come locked and loaded if I knew this was happening."

Epps asked the man to move back away from police.

"Take a step back," he said on video broadcast by Just Another Channel. "We're holding ground. We're not trying to get people hurt. They don't want to get hurt, you don't want to get hurt. Back off."

Clark said he is determined to take his Jan. 6 charges to trial, and if he loses, he will serve the time.

"I'll sit in solitary confinement some year—ain't nothing," he said. "I deserve that for crimes that I committed as a heroin and meth addict that I got away with. Not sweating their three years."" The Epoch Times, June 28, 2022. 'Ray Epps was Worried Jan 6 Crowd Might Interfere With 'The Plan'... ' by Joseph Hanneman.

Evidence now proves that "plainclothes" members of a special **Electronic Surveillance Unit (ESU)** of the Capitol Police were embedded among the protesters for the purposes of conducting video surveillance.

Criminal defense lawyers to the rescue! (May 11, 2022)

"Defense attorneys are seeking to identify and investigate 80 "suspicious actors" and material witnesses, some of whom allegedly ran an entrapment operation against the Oath Keepers on Jan. 6, 2021, and committed crimes including the removal of security fencing, breaching police lines, attacking officers, and inciting crowds to storm into the U.S. Capitol. Suspicious actors are seen on video "associating, conferring and traveling with others, engaging in behavior to confuse law enforcement through body masking, facial masking, clothing changes, and disorienting skirmishing behavior," Geyer wrote.

The suspected people used earpieces, satellite phones, and other communication equipment.

"Often it appears that these communications devices do not seem to be affected by capacity restriction or sophisticated jamming that was evident throughout the day," Geyer wrote in the motion.

"If it can be established that these SAs [suspicious actors] were government agents, this could amount to entrapment defense that will dispose of this 7th indictment prior to trial," the motion says."

FBI plants (Reported Jan 20, 2022)

"Most of the men who attacked the Speaker's Lobby doors at the U.S. Capitol on Jan. 6, 2021, have **NOT** been identified or arrested, and the family of Ashli Babbitt wants to question them about the events that led up to her shooting death. Of the dozens of people who congregated before the double doors leading from the hallway into the Speaker's Lobby that day, only two have been arrested by the FBI. The Babbitt family has identified at least six others who could have valuable information on what took place before and after U.S. Capitol Police Lt. Michael Byrd shot and killed Babbitt. Aaron Babbitt said identifying these men is an important part of his investigation into his wife's killing. He said the authorities are not interested in pursuing it."

Ray Epps (Reported Dec 20, 2021)

"Ray Epps's name (was he an informant?) was purged from the FBI files.

Some 700 people have been arrested for their part in the Jan. 6 demonstration.

But Epps and a handful of other major players in that drama remain unindicted.

Indeed, although the FBI surely knows their identity, they remain nameless to the public, known only through amateur video footage of the event.

Hence their colorful soubriquets: "ScaffoldCommander," "FenceCutterBulwark," "BlackSkiMask," and so on.

Beattie shows that what the media label an "insurrection" is almost certainly better described as a "Fedsurrection." Beattie shows how other actors calmly removed fences and signage on Jan. 6, clearing a path for the protesters, who were carefully funneled through that one walkway up to the Capitol.

"Okay we're in!" shouted the man known as "Scaffold Commander," so-called because he was perched, megaphone in hand, atop a tall tower overlooking the Capitol complex.

"We're in!" he shouted. "Come on! We gotta fill up the Capitol! Come on! Come now! We need help. We gotta fill up the Capitol! They got in."

Will coincidences never end? The blue and white megaphone he was using was identical to the blue and white megaphones used by other people directing the crowd.

Beattie (from Revolver News) isn't the only person to notice the oddity of it all. This Twitter thread, published the day after the event: "What happened yesterday was not as it seemed."

Indeed.

"What makes the ScaffoldCommander-Ray Epps affair complete," Beattie noted, "is that they appeared to work in tandem from start to finish the entire day on 1/6.

"Both set up positions at the initial 12:50 p.m. 'Big Bang' breach site, and they did so before the Proud Boys arrived.

"The official story, you will recall, says that the Proud Boys group caused the riot."

Ray Epps (Reported Dec 2, 2021)

From Revolver: "Ray Epps. Did he work for the FBI? The CIA? ….. He confessed on camera to plotting a pre-planned 'event' on the Capitol. Yet he has never been arrested? Why not? 'Unindicted conspirators' almost always work for the FBI, the CIA or some other agency. 'On January 5th and 6th Epps announced multiple times, at multiple location, his upcoming plot to breach the US Capitol. He then spent hours attempting to recruit hundreds of others to join him. On top of it all, Epps was seen leading key people and managing key aspects of the Capitol grounds itself.' From video clips, you can see Epps actively orchestrate elements of the first breach of the Capitol barricades at 12:50 pm, while Trump still had 20 minutes left in his rally speech.' …… 'Epps breach occurs just one minute after Capitol police began responding to two reports of two pipe bombs located at DNC and GOP headquarters.' So the police would have less resources to respond to the protestors. … The NYT, WSJ and DOJ all depict the Ray Epps orchestrated initial breach of the metal barricades as the 'Big Bang' of January 6. …. On Jan 8 the FBI listed Epps on its website as #16 in its list of highest targets, out of 500. … On June 30, 2020, the FBI purged all references to Epps from its website. The FBI's posture towards Epps: 'Who? What? Ray Epps? Never heard of him.' "… (Source: Revolver).

Ray Epps (Reported Nov 20, 2021)

"Ray Epps pretended he was a Trump supporter and wore a Trump red baseball hat when he went to the Capitol Building on Jan 6. He was on video telling people to break into the Capitol. The crowd yelled 'No, No,' ' 'Fed, Fed,'. Epps has never been charged. The FBI knows where he lives. The FBI have arrested 68 year old grandmothers who were difficult to identify and who did not harm anyone or any property and did not instigate anything. Why has Epps not been arrested? Is he an FBI agent or informant?

But they didn't.

A review of the video footage shows a handful of main players that day.

None have been indicted.

Why?

The simplest explanation is that the people who took down the fences and the "restricted area" signs, who loudly directed the crowd into the Capitol, were federal assets.

Beattie is right.

"If Ray Epps was acting on instructions from a government handler from any federal agency (FBI, ATF, Pentagon, DHS, DEA, anything), we now are talking about perhaps the single most egregious caught-on-camera intelligence operation in our lifetimes." The Epoch Times 'Jan 6' by Roger Kimball.

FBI agents posed at Trump supporters at Jan 6 (Reported Oct 21, 2021)

DOJ head Garland testified to Congress that FBI agents posed as Trump supporters at the Jan 6 protest, but he refused to say how many. Fox News, Oct 21, 2021.

THE MICHIGAN KIDNAPPING PLOT AND THE FBI

A ridiculous talking point of the Democrats and their legacy media minions was that Trump and his voters supported violent right wing groups. Dems etc repeated this lie in order to scare soccer moms and independents into not voting for Trump or Republicans. They also did it because it is in their nature to be nasty, vindictive and because of their insatiable quest for power.

A Democrat connected group, The Lincoln Project, dressed up six guys to look like white supremacists, holding torches, and wearing red Trump hats, and standing as a group at a Republican candidate for governor of Virginia, Youngkin's rally. They got caught, and the scum at the Lincoln Project admitted the set up. Democrats routinely show up at Republican rallies posing as Republicans, waiving confederate flags and wearing anti-semitic t-shirts. They brag on Facebook that they do this. Democrat Jesse Smollett claimed in highly Dem Chicago he was punched in the face by two Trump supporters who yelled, "This is MAGA country!" and he said they poured bleach in his face, and put a noose around his neck -- but in fact the two were his friends from Nigeria, and he paid them. In 2017, 3 separate Muslim young ladies said they were attacked by Trump supporters. They all admitted they had lied, and they were arrested for filing false police reports. AOC made a highly emotional and theatric video about how she thought she was going to be killed by Trump supporters while she was in the Capitol Building on January 6. Then she was captured on video in a building far from the Capitol that day. She then admitted that she had lied. All this shows the Dem's false flag operation falsely linking Republicans to violent right wing groups. How does all of this connect the Dems to the FBI?

The FBI promulgated this lie, this lie that the biggest danger to the country was right wing groups, because it helped Biden and the Dems.

What's the proof of this assertion? The FBI has never offered a single piece of evidence that this is true. Where are the FBI's studies and statistics and proof. No where. They do not exist. The FBI is one giant misinformation operation. Moreover, how many times have you seen the news report a right wing group that was violent? Never. There were 520 BLM related violent protests in the summer of 2020, all left wing. ANITFA was involved in many. The two weeks of violent protests outside the Trump White House in the summer of 2020 were all by Dems. The tearing down of statues was all by Dems. The raiding of Judge Kavanaugh Senate confirmation hearings were all by Dems. The storming of the Department of the Interior was by Dems. The throwing of paint on works of art was all by Dems. The 80 burnings and attacks on pro-life pregnancy centers were all by Dems. And the FBI arrested almost no one for this violence, and those arrested were given very light sentences.

As an example of the FBI's lie about right wing groups, there was the fake plot to kidnap the governor of Michigan, as described below.

INTRODUCTION

The FBI couldn't find any right wing nationalists even though Biden was using that as a talking point in his campaign. Biden was saying, 'The greatest threat to our Democracy are domestic terrorists.' Oh yea Joe, worse than 9/11 or the Orlando night club massacre under Obama?

Of course this isn't true. When was the last time you have seen domestic terrorists on the news (except of course, attendees at the Democratic National Convention)? But the FBI is in the Bidens' pocket.

So the FBI had to create domestic terrorists. They framed a group of innocent and fairly docile guys hanging out in the basement of a vacuum repair shop in Michigan by trying to get the guys to kidnap the governor. The FBI made the kidnap plans, trained the guys and paid for their travel and hotel rooms. They even had a female agent sleep with one of the guys to further the plot.

Then when the plan backfired, the same FBI chief went to DC to frame the Jan 6 protesters. Nice guys, these FBI guys.

FBI PLOT TO FRAME ORDINARY AMERICANS FOR THE KIDNAPPING

Dear FBI - why don't you just plant cocaine instead? That would be easier.

The FBI tried to entrap six guys into kidnapping Governor Whitmer of Michigan. Two were acquitted - Daniel Harris and Brandon Caserta. Two others got a mistrial. New York Post, April 9, 2022, 'Whitmer Duo Acquit,' by Callie Patteson. …. An update - Two other guys did get convicted in August 2022. They will likely appeal.

Details of the FBI frame job

"A supposed terrorism plot was in fact a setup by the government to make a bunch of ordinary looking people in Michigan look like terrifying right wing extremists. Those violent right wing nationalists Joe Biden is always mumbling about. It turns out there aren't enough of those people in real life. They are pretty rare. It's not a very racist country despite what they tell you.

So the Justice Dept had to go create some. And they did. That was the finding of a Federal jury in Michigan.

The details of the story are beyond belief. There was a trial and a re-trial, and the facts below came out of the evidence presented at the trial.

The FBI engineered the plot. Here's an outline:

Names of FBI agents and informants: Dan Chappel, Jason Chambers, Steven Robson, Richard Traff, Steven DeAntrono

Names of victims, ie FBI targets: Adam Fox, Barry Croft, Daniel Harrison

In early 2020 a 35 year old army veteran named Dan Chappal nicknamed Big Dan was working as a contractor for the US Postal service. He was scrolling Facebook one night and he ran across a pro 2nd amendment group called 'Wolverine Watchman.' Chappal was worried they might be violent, so he went to a police friend of his who connected him to the FBI. None of the chat was illegal. An FBI agent named Jason Chambers got involved.

Jason Chambers was interested in the case because in addition to being an agent, he had a side hustle. He had a security firm called EXE Intel. This violated FBI rules. He saw his work on the Whitmer case as a way to promote his own business. Someone in his business had repeatedly tweeted nonpublic information about the kidnapping case that Dan Chappel was building for the FBI. So Chambers did everything he could so the investigation went according to plan. No investigation can go according to plan because there shouldn't be a plan. An investigation is the process of finding out what happened, but not the process to orchestrate something *to happen*. But that is exactly what this became.

Chambers as the handler paid Chappel the informant, 'Bi Dan', more than $60,000 just in the course of just a few months. Chappel testified he made more in 6 months from the FBI than he made from the Postal Service over the course of an entire year.

So the FBI told Chappel in exchange for all that money he needed to *start assembling* a group of right wing extremists for the FBI to prosecute. They made the whole thing up. And he did that with the FBI's help.

Within a few weeks the FBI created a new Facebook group called

'Patriot 3 percenters.' (So be careful about Facebook groups. 'It's just a group. It looks interesting'). So Chappel then attended a protest at the Michigan capitol. The FBI texted Chappel, "Looking you bringing people together." During the protest he informed the FBI that a 37-year-old man named Adam Fox was at the protest.

Adam Fox is one of the least powerful people in US society. He lived alone with his 2 dogs in the basement of a vacuum cleaner repair shop. He had no money. In order to get hot water he had to go to a nearby Mexican restaurant and use their men's room.

So Chappel began texting ' this diabolical mastermind Fox' hundreds of times. But Fox seemed inherently moderate. He wrote things like "Our goal is to restore the constitutional republic." "In our hearts and minds, we are not domestic terrorists."

Based on those test messages, the FBI gave Chappel more instructions. They provided Chappel with several $5,000 limit credit cards, and they told Chappel to give them to Fox, and to tell Fox to buy guns and ammunition. So Fox refused the cards. On five separate occasions he refused to take the credit cards to buy guns and ammunition.

Then in July of 2020 Chappel suggested to Fox and others to fire rounds into the governor's mansion as well at her cottage. But the alleged plotters including Adam Fox again refused. They didn't want to hurt the governor.

In August 2020 the group began to splinter. The FBI told Chappel to keep the group together. "Keep the threat real."

The FBI then introduced another under undercover agent who pretended to be an explosive expert. He showed the group a bomb blowing up a vehicle to prove he knew what he was doing. Where did the video come from? It was made by the FBI.

Then the FBI brought in a convicted felon and long time FBI informant named Steven Robson to introduce a new idea to Fox and a guy named Barry Croft. This time the idea was to kidnap Gretchen Whitmer. Robson used FBI money to organize several events including a national militia conference in Ohio, a training event in

Wisconsin, and a meeting in Delaware. The FBI orchestrated all of this. On July 18, 2020 at one such militia meeting, again organized by the FBI, an alleged plotter named Ty Garbon rejected out of hand to idea to kidnap Gretchen Whitmer. Then the topic came up again in August. Another guy there named Daniel Harris said, "No snatch and grab. I swear to F'n God." These are people who clearly did not want to kidnap Whitmer.

The FBI kept pushing. The FBI informants drove the defendants to Whitmer's home, and they also suggested killing the Democrat governor of Virgina.

On September 5, 2020 FBI special agent Jason Chambers texted Chappel, "Mission is to kill the governor specifically."

To pressure on of the defendants, Barry Croft, one FBI agent admitted at the trial on Aug 16, 2022 that a female FBI informant slept in the same hotel room as Croft. It was a honeytrap.

FBI agents also testified on August 16, 2022 that they regularly got high with Adam Fox. They said he was so high, in fact he was so high in all of his meeting with them. This is against FBI policy. You can't give drugs to someone and hope they do something bad.

All of this failed to produce a kidnapping plot. So another FBI agent named Richard Traff arrived to set up a new plot to kidnap Whitmer. That same year Traff he been charged with beating his wife. He had called Donald Trump, 'a piece of shit' on Facebook / Twitter.

The FBI supervisor for this frame job, Steven DeAntrono, was promoted to run the FBI DC field office in late 2020. But don't ask if the FBI used informants on Jan 6 to entrap people. Also don't ask if DeAntrono's agents were involved in the raid on Mar-A-Lago, even though he's in DC, not Florida. Questions like these are 'hate speech' per Morning Joe and his wife on MSNBC. They are really saying you are committing a crime.

It is beyond question that the FBI tried to create an act of terror in Michigan."

Source: Derived from Tucker Carlson, Fox News, August 16, 2022.

***

FBI planted explosives to frame a guy

"The FBI informant planted explosives material in truck of defendant so FBI could confiscate the evidence upon arrest." One of the defense lawyers in the Governor Whitmer FBI frame job tweeted this week. Aug 10, 2022. Julie Kelly tweet.

FBI, we know you're guilty

The FBI Investigation into Alleged Michigan Governor Kidnapping Plot Is a Mess The case seemed like a lock — until an informant and one FBI agent were charged with crimes, another was accused of perjury, and a third was found promoting a private security firm. And that wasn't all. Buzzfeednews, Dec 16, 2021, 'The FBI Said It Busted a Plot To Kidnap Michigan's Governor. Then Things Got Complicated.' By Ken Bensinger and Jessica Garrison.

THE FBI HAS A SLEAZY PAST

The vast majority of FBI agents and employees are great people defending the USA, and our democracy. Fantastic, loyal, moral people. …. Then there is the scum at the top, and some dirtbags in the rank and file. Below describes some of the criminals and sleaze who have worked at the bureau.

*   *   *

In February 2023 "a former senior FBI counterintelligence official who reportedly was involved in the Trump-Russia probe was arrested and charged over his own alleged ties to a sanctioned Russian oligarch amid the war in Ukraine.

"Charles McGonigal, the former special agent in charge of the FBI's Counterintelligence Division in New York who retired in 2018, is charged with violating U.S. sanctions by agreeing to provide services to Oleg Deripaska, a sanctioned Russian oligarch. He was charged alongside Sergey Shestakov, a former Soviet and Russian diplomat who later became a U.S. citizen and a Russian interpreter for courts and government offices, through a five-count indictment unsealed in Manhattan federal court Monday.[31]"

*   *   *

The following is a list of various sleazy FBI employees:

Earl Edwin Pitts Dec 18, 1986 convicted committing espionage for Russia …… Mark Putnam June 8, 1989 convicted of manslaughter ….. Dan Mitrione Jr March 1993 convicted of taking bribes, payoffs from

---

[31] Danielle Wallace, Fox News, February 2023,

drug deals …. Robert Hanssen Feb 18, 2001 charged with committing espionage for Russia provided highly classified antional security info, still in jail, Russians still killing people he provided info on ….Leandro Aragoncillo June 16, 2007 convicted of committing espionage for the Philippines …… John Connolly Jr 2011 convicted of racketeering , obstruction of justice, murder, he did contract killings for the mobster Whitey Bulger …. Robert Lustyik March 30, 2015 convicted of bribery, obstruction scheme, wire fraud …. Christopher Bauer May 10, 2021 charged with sodomy and sexual abuse of child under 12 allegedly ….. Amberly Boyle Aug 25, 2021 charged with domestic abuse battery ….. David Harris charged with sex crimes with minors across three states …. Eduardo Valdivia Dec 15, 2021 charged with attempted murder, assault, reckless endangerment …. Kenneth Diu April 19, 2022 charged with assault, tampering with records, obstruction …. Richard Trask aggravated assault …. Carlos Ortiz lethal threats …. James Smith Chinese espionage…. Richard Miller Russian espionage ….. Mark Rossini corruption …. Terry Albury Document leak … Babak Broumand conspiracy ,,,, Chase Bishop assault … Joseph Astarita false claims under oath …. Ruben Hernandez assault … Matthey Lowry drug trafficking …. Donal Sachleben child pornography…. And more. Newsmax, Gregg Kelly, Aug 15, 2022.

FBI not following their own regulations (re Hunter)

An FBI whistleblower has reported that the FBI shut down the investigation into Hunter's laptop without giving a reason, as required by FBI regulations. Fox News, Tucker Carlson, July 27, 2022.

Guy in prison for 20 years because of FBI sleaze

Because of FBI lying, Mahammad Aziz and another guy spent 20 years in prison, where they were falsely accused of killing Malcom X. The FBI withheld critical evidence that would have likely exonerated Aziz, and so a judge tossed the convictions. He has sued for $40 million. …. He should up that amount. New York Post, July 14, 2022, by Ben Feuerherd

* * *

Gymnasts sue the FBI for one billion $$

A group of women US gymnasts have sued the FBI for one billion, yes billion, dollars, for knowing that the team doctor was sexually assaulting the women, and not doing anything about it. May 2022.

An ongoing Democrat war on women

Pregnancy centers assist women when they are pregnant. They help the newborn and the mother. Dems hate these centers: Pro-Abortion group 'Jane's Revenge' has firebombed or attacked 20 pregnancy centers. …. The FBI does nothing. … Garland and the DOJ do nothing. … Meanwhile, the FBI had sent 7 agents to a NASCAR garage to look at a loop in a rope on a garage door in 2021. June 2022.

Oklahoma City Bombing - FBI involvement?

The FBI had some type of involvement with the Oklahoma City Bombing of 1995. Attorney Jesse Trentadue has filed a FOI suite and the FBI and CIA have been fighting it since 2015. The FBI has a Patriot Conspiracy program (PATCON) whose purpose is to infiltrate and incite fringe groups. Trentadue states the FBI is suppressing video. 24 witnesses told the FBI they saw McVeigh (one of the bombers) with someone the morning of the bombings, but none were used at the trial. The FBI released sketches of the persons and asked the public for help to find him, and then later denied the man ever existed. FBI informant Matthews was to testify in the FOI case but the FBI intimidated him not to according to Trentadue – the FBI told Matthew to 'stand down', take a vacation at the time of the trial, and that he would lose his VA benefits and veteran's pension. The Epoch Times, Feb 23, 2022, 'FBI Operation to Infiltrate Extremist Groups Center of Historic Lawsuit, by Ken Silva.

MLK and FBI

The FBI spied on Martin Luther King, sought sex tapes on him, and leaked info.

FBI malfeasance and incompetence

The New York Post listed FBI malfeasance and incompetence (New York Post, Nov 19, 2021, "How the FBI Went Bad" by Victor Davis Hanson):

"Investigating and tracking parents who confront school boards.

FBI head Lying Jimmy Comey allowed H Clinton's private computer contractor, CrowdStrike, to run the investigation of the hack and keep possession of hard drives associated with it.

During Robert Mueller's special investigation the FBI "implausibly claimed it had no idea how requested information on cell phones mysteriously disappeared."

Under Comey the FBI submitted lies in requests for warrants to the FISA court.

FBI lawyer Kevin Clinesman forged elements of an affidavit to surveil Trump aid Carter Page. Good old Kevin boy changed it from "Page worked for the CIA" to Page DID NOT work for the CIA. A 100 percent change. I believe Kevin still works for the FBI (why?). He pleaded guilty.

The FBI hired lying and disreputable ex-British spy Christopher Steele as a contractor while he was peddling fantasies.

"Former FBI General Counsel James Baker was reportedly the subject of a federal investigation for meetings with media outlets that later leaked lurid tales from the Steele dossier. He also met repeatedly with now indicted Perkins Coe attorney Michael Sussman."

Comey admitted he leaked his confidential memos detailing his private meetings with President Trump, The Great, The Orangeman.

"In sworn testimony to Congress Comey on 245 occasions claimed he could not remember or had no knowledge of key elements of his own 'Russian Collusion' investigation."

FBI Comey replacement Andrew 'The Dick' McCabe was fired for leaking sensitive information to the so called 'Media. He lied on at least 3 occasions to federal attorneys and his own FBI investigators. Now on CNN he offers misleading information on the Russian hoax he helped promulgate.

Mueller testified to Congress that he 'claimed' he had little or no knowledge about Fusion GI's or the Steele Dossier – the sources that birthed the entire collusion hoax. ... What a LIAR ... or a doddering old alzheimer infected idiot ... or a guy who acts like an alzheimer idiot, but is really a flim-flam man who is pretending to be a fool so he and his family can scam us all, and make tons of money

The FBI sent a huge swat team to Ft Lauderdale to arrest a 70 year old man with no criminal record, and with no reason to believe he was violent. Oh, they were afraid of his 70 year old wife? They even had a gun boat in the canal behind the house. The man was Roger Stone, of course. ... Wimps. ... Oh, and they contacted CNN first so the douche bags could be on the scene to film the morons (the FBI agents that is).

The FBI stormed the house of Project Veritas head James O'Keefe to do the personal work of Joe Biden, getting his daughter's diary back. ... This action of Biden's is the crime of 'stealing government' resources" since the FBI work was for personal benefits, such as using city public works people to install a hot tub at your house while they are on city worktime.

The FBI did not disclose that it possessed Hunter B's laptop, while the main stream media declared the NY Post reporting on was Russian disinformation.

US Olympic doctor Lasser Nassar was a known and chronic child molester. The perverts at the FBI downed-played the evidence. Several gymnasts have sued the FBI over this.

12 FBI agents or informants had leadership roles in the in the kidnapping scheme of Michigan governor Gretchen Whitmer."

* * *

The FBI stated they only track right wing 'violent' groups, and not left wing 'violent' groups. Left wing groups caused 527 violent riots in 2020. Oct. 3, 2021.

McCabe: FBI criminal lies, keeps his pension, and gets a gig on CNN

FBI liar Andrew McCabe got his pension back and a lot of legal fees, per an order from Biden's DOJ. AG Sessions under Trump fired him. The DOJ Inspector General report called him a 'serial liar', gave details and recommended he be fired for lack of candor. He also signed the bogus and politically motivated FISA warrant used to illegally spy on Trump campaign advisor Carter Page. He lied multiple times while under oath to the IG and to FBI investigators. He improperly leaked sensitive info to the Wall Street Journal and then lied about it to FBI director James Comey. Katie Pavlich of Town Hall, October 15, 2021. .... Why did Barr not prosecute him? Roger Stone and General Flynn were prosecuted for much smaller transgressions. How about the two 67 year old ladies who were prosecuted for walking around the Capital Building for 15 minutes and causing no violence nor property damage on Jan 6? Huh??

More FBI entrapments

It has also been revealed that the FBI may have encouraged or entrapped many otherwise peaceful people to do violent acts. Shahawar Matin Siraj in attempting to bomb New York's Herald Square. And Boston police believe the FBI is protecting whoever made the bombs for the Marathon bombers, the Tsarnaevs. The FBI encouraged a Muslim man to kill several Dallas police officers. An FBI agent was arrested at the scene. The head of the FBI, Christopher Wrey did not deny that the FBI had infiltrated the January 6 crowd. New York Post, July 25, 2021.

* * *

FBI: 'Yea Dr. Nassar, you can sexually assault young girls. We don't care.'

The FBI knew for years that Dr. Nassar, the gymnast coach was sexually assaulting young female gymnasts, and the FBI did nothing!! … How many lives did the FBI ruin?

Another whistleblower has reported that the FBI is juicing the books to fraudulently make their stats on domestic extremism higher than they really are in order to fraudulently support Biden's false story that domestic terro

FBI Kavanaugh tip line

Per an FBI letter to the Senate: Justice Kavanaugh's nomination "was the first time that the FBI set-up a tip line for a nominee undergoing Senate confirmation," and that tip line received "over 4,500 tips. Source: Senator (RI) Whitehouse's website. July 2022.

FBI spies on Trump

The FBI spied on the Trump Campaign in 2016, using the fake Steel dossier as a pretext, knowing the dossier was all lies and fabrications.

Comey screws his boss

Comey met with Trump about the Steel dossier even though Comey knew it was a total fabrication. He did the meeting because doing so allowed him to release the fake dossier to the press.

'Ha ha ha, we got them.' Comey

Comey said in an interview that he knew he was breaking White

House protocol by sending 2 agents to interview General Flynn without first clearing the meeting with White House counsel. Comey laughed about it, and bragged. A crime??

Two systems of justices. Barr, why did you fail to prosecute?

"One of Justice Brett M. Kavanaugh's accusers admitted this week that she made up her lurid tale of a backseat car rape, saying it "was a tactic" to try to derail the judge's confirmation to the Supreme Court. Sen. Chuck Grassley, chairman of the Judiciary Committee revealed the fraud in a letter to the FBI and Justice Department Friday, asking them to prosecute Judy Munro-Leighton for lying to and obstructing Congress. Mr. Grassley's investigators tried to reach her for a month but were unsuccessful until this week, when they spoke to her by phone and she confessed that she was not the original Jane Doe, and "did that as a way to grab attention." The FBI did nothing. Associated Press , Nov 3, 2018, 'Kavanaugh accuser admits to making up rape allegation ...' by Stephan Dinan.

Agents erase texts

Two FBI agents connected to the FBI's involvement with the Russian hoax erased the texts on their cell phones. They worked for special prosecutor Mueller. He did nothing to them. This is a crime. 'Obstruction of Justice.' 2018.

WHY no prosecution, Barr? False Kavanaugh accuser, Rhode Island boat rape claim

"A Rhode Island man who claimed U.S. Supreme Court nominee Brett Kavanaugh sexually assaulted a woman aboard a boat in Rhode Island more than 30 years ago apologized Wednesday, saying he "made a mistake." The FBI did nothing.

Strzok to his FBI lover, "It's an insurance policy"

FBI lawyer Lisa Paige asked her FBI lover Peter Strzok, 'Trump will never become president, will he?' Strzok said, 'No. No he's not. *We'll* stop it.' Later he said, 'It's like an insurance policy' we have against him becoming president. Strzok never faced legal consequences.

Lock her up!

FBI head James Comey said Hillary Clint's actions regarding her emails and server were criminal conduct, but she did not 'have an intent to commit a crime.' He said, 'No prosecutor would bring charges.' As a result, he said what she did was not a crime! ... Plus, it was not Comey's decision to make. It was the AG's, Lynch. And Lynch then could have still prosecuted Clinton, but instead she just relied on Comey so that Lynch was not put in a position of having to clear Clinton. .... Compare this to what the FBI did to General Flynn. The field agents said that Flynn did not lie to them, and the case was being closed until the criminal McCabe reopened it, and prosecuted Flynn. 2016.

The secret service hides Hunter's gun purchase fraudulent records

The secret service improperly confiscated Hunter's gun purchase records from the the seller, which showed he had lied to get the gun by saying he did not take drugs. The secret service is not supposed to act as a private citizen's baby sitter.

FBI terrorizes an innocent NJ woman

The FBI sent *three* agents to a woman's home, Lisa Gallagher, in NJ to ask her if she was in DC during Jan 6. She was not. She had to pull out old calendars to prove it to the thugs. The FBI thugs went to her house in response to an 'anonymous tip.' Tucker Carlson, Sept 12,

2022 ... do you think the FBI will arrest the tipster? FBI - why don't you devote agents to the fentanyl mass murders and the pregnancy fire bombings, you worthless scum.

A FBI supervisory intelligence analyst in Utah was charged with molesting multiple children. Aug 2022.

*   *   *

"May 14, 2001 -- Two families who claim their lives were destroyed by two Massachusetts mob figures-turned-FBI informants said they plan to sue the Boston FBI for $600 million.

"Attorneys for the families of slain Oklahoma millionaire Roger Wheeler and South Boston liquor store owner Stephen Rakes claim the FBI is responsible for Wheeler's shooting death and the extortion of Rakes.

"Both crimes, the attorneys say, were orchestrated by longtime FBI informants — and reputed Boston organized crime lords — James "Whitey" Bulger and Stephen "The Rifleman" Flemmi.

""These are two law-abiding families from different walks of life whose lives were destroyed by two known criminals and killers and the FBI could have foreseen it," attorney Paul Kelly said today. "They [FBI officials] knew the potential danger these men posed to these families and did nothing to prevent it.""[32]

*   *   *

---

[32] Bryan Robinson, "Familes sue FBI for $600 million," *ABC News.com,* May 14, 2001.

THE FBI USED TWITTER TO CENSOR ON BEHALF OF THE DEMOCRATS AND PELOSI

When Elon Musk took over Twitter, he released internal Twitter documents revealing the FBI's interaction with Twitter on behalf of the Democrats, and thus on behalf of Pelosi. The Twitter files give further evidence of the FBI's collusion with the Democrats, and thus with Pelosi. It is more circumstantial evidence that the FBI's instigation of the Capitol Building break-in can be connected to Pelosi.

From The Epoch Times:

"Elon Musk's takeover of Twitter last October and the subsequent reporting on the Twitter Files by journalists Matt Taibbi, Bari Weiss, and a handful of others beginning in early December is one of the most important news stories of our time.

"The Twitter Files story encompasses, and to a large extent connects, every major political scandal of the Trump–Biden era. Put simply, the Twitter Files reveal an unholy alliance between Big Tech and the deep state designed to throttle free speech and maintain an official narrative through censorship and propaganda. This should not just disturb us, it should also prod us to action in defense of the First Amendment, free and fair elections, and indeed our country.

"After Musk completed his acquisition of Twitter, he fired a slew of useless or insubordinate employees, instituted new content moderation policies, and tried to reform a "woke" corporate culture that bordered (and still borders) on parody.

"In the process, Musk coordinated with Taibbi and Weiss on the publication of a series of stories based on internal Twitter documents related to an array of major political events going back years: the Hunter Biden laptop scandal, Twitter's secret policy of shadow banning, President Trump's suspension from Twitter after the January

6 U.S. Capitol riot, the co-opting of Twitter by the FBI to suppress "election disinformation" ahead of the 2020 election, Twitter's involvement in a Pentagon overseas psy-op campaign, its silencing of dissent from the official COVID narrative, its complicity in the Russiagate hoax, and its gradual capitulation to the direct involvement of the U.S. intelligence community—with the FBI as a go-between—in content moderation.

"As Taibbi has written, the Twitter Files "show the FBI acting as doorman to a vast program of social media surveillance and censorship, encompassing agencies across the federal government—from the State Department to the Pentagon to the CIA."

"The Twitter Files contain multitudes, but for the sake of brevity let us consider just three installments and their related implications: the suppression of the Hunter Biden laptop story, the suspension of Trump, and the deputization of Twitter by the FBI. Together, these stories reveal not just a social media company willing to do the bidding of an out-of-control federal bureaucracy, but a federal bureaucracy openly hostile to the First Amendment.

Hunter Biden's Laptop

"On Oct. 14, 2020, the New York Post published its first major exposé based on the contents of Hunter Biden's laptop, which had been dropped off at a Delaware computer repair shop in April 2019 and never picked up. It wasthe first of several stories detailing Biden family corruption and revealing the close involvement of Joe Biden in his son's foreign business ventures in the years during and after Biden's vice presidency. Hunter, although doing no real work, was making tens of millions of dollars from foreign companies in places like Ukraine and China. The Post's bombshell reporting shined a bright light on what was happening.

"According to emails on the laptop, Hunter introduced then-Vice President Biden to a top executive at Burisma, a Ukrainian energy company that was paying Hunter (who had no credentials or experience in the energy business) up to $50,000 a month to sit on its board. Soon after this meeting, Vice President Biden pressured the Ukrainian government to fire a prosecutor investigating the company.

In an earlier email, a top Burisma executive asked Hunter for "advice on how [he]could use [his]influence" to benefit the company.

"The Post's ensuing stories revealed more of the same: a shocking level of corruption and influence-peddling by Hunter Biden, whose emails suggest his father was closely connected to his overseas business ventures. Indeed, those ventures appear to consist entirely of Hunter providing access to Joe Biden.

"Twitter did everything in its power to suppress the Biden story. It removed links to the Post's reporting, appended warnings that they might be "unsafe," and prevented users from sharing them via direct message—a restriction previously reserved for child pornography and other extreme cases. In an extraordinary step, Twitter also locked the Post's account and the accounts of anyone who shared links to its reporting, including White House press secretary Kayleigh McEnany. [The justification provided for] these actions [was] the pretext that the stories violated Twitter's hacked-materials policy, even though there was no evidence that anything on the laptop was hacked.

"Twitter executives at the highest levels were directly involved in these decisions. Former head of legal, policy, and trust Vijaya Gadde, the company's chief censor, played a key role, as did former head of trust and safety Yoel Roth. Oddly, all this seems to have been done without the knowledge of Twitter's then-CEO Jack Dorsey. And it was done despite internal pushback from other departments.

""I'm struggling to understand the policy basis for marking this as unsafe," wrote a Twitter communications executive in an email to Gadde and Roth. "Can we truthfully claim that this is part of the policy?" asked former VP of Global Communications Brandon Borman. His question was answeredby Deputy General Counsel Jim Baker—a former top lawyer for the FBI and the most powerful member of a growing cadre of former FBI employees working at Twitter—who said that "caution is warranted" and that some facts "indicate the materials may have been hacked."

"But there were no such facts, as Baker and other top Twitter executives knew at the time. The laptop was exactly what the Post said it was, and every fact the Post reported was accurate. Other major media outlets like The New York Times and The Washington Post would begrudgingly admit as much 18 months later, after Joe Biden was ensconced in the White House.

"If there were no hacked materials in the Post's reporting, why did Twitter immediately react as if there were? Because long before the Post published its first laptop story, there had been an organized effort by the intelligence community to discredit leaked information about Hunter Biden. The laptop, after all, had been in federal custody since the previous December, when the FBI seized it from the computer repair shop. So the FBI knew very well that it contained evidence of straightforward criminal activity, such as illicit drug use, as well as of corruption and influence-peddling.

"The evening before the Post ran its first story on the laptop, FBI special agent Elvis Chan sent 10 documents to Roth at Twitter through a special one-way communications channel the FBI had established with the company. For months, the FBI and other federal intelligence agencies had been priming Roth to dismiss news reports about Hunter Biden ahead of the 2020 election as "hack-and-leak" operations by state actors. They had done the same thing with Facebook, whose CEO, Mark Zuckerberg, admitted as much to Joe Rogan in an August 2022 podcast.

"As Michael Shellenberger reported in the seventh installment of the Twitter Files, the FBI repeatedly asked Roth and others at Twitter about foreign influence operations on the platform and were repeatedly told there were none of any significance. The FBI also routinely pressured Twitter to hand over data outside the normal search warrant process, which Twitter at first resisted.

"In July 2020, Chan arranged for Twitter executives to get top secret security clearances so the FBI could share intelligence about possible threats to the upcoming presidential election. The next month, Chan sent Roth information about a Russian hacking group called APT28.

"Roth later said [about the Post's story about Hunter Biden's laptop], "It set off every single one of my finely tuned APT28 hack-and-leak campaign alarm bells."

"Even though there was never any evidence that anything on the laptop was hacked, Roth reacted to it just as the FBI had conditioned him to do, using the company's hacked-materials policy to suppress the story as soon as it appeared, just as the agency suggested it would, less than a month before the election.

Suspending the President

"The erosion of Twitter's content moderation standards would continue after the Hunter Biden laptop scandal, reaching its apogee on Jan. 8, 2021, two days after the Capitol [breach]. That is when Twitter made the extraordinary decision to suspend President Trump, even though he had not violated any Twitter policies. As the Twitter Files show, the suspension came amid ongoing interactions with federal agencies—interactions that were increasing in frequency in the months leading up to the 2020 election. Roth was meeting weekly with the FBI, the Department of Homeland Security, and the Office of the Director of National Intelligence. As the election neared, Twitter's unevenly applied, rules-based content moderation policies would steadily deteriorate.

"Content moderation on Twitter had always been an unstable mix of automatic enforcement of rules and subjective interventions by top executives, most of whom used Twitter's censorship tools to diminish the reach of Trump and others on the right through shadow banning and other means. But that was changing. As Taibbi wrote in the third installment of the Twitter Files: "As the election approached, senior executives—perhaps under pressure from federal agencies, with whom they met more as time progressed—increasingly struggled with rules, and began to speak of 'vios' [violations] as pretexts to do what they'd likely have done anyway."

"After Jan. 6, Twitter jettisoned even the appearance of a rules-based moderation policy, suspending Trump for a pair of tweets that top executives falsely claimed were violations of Twitter's terms of service. The first, sent early in the morning on Jan. 8, stated: "The 75,000,000 great American Patriots who voted for me, AMERICA FIRST, and MAKE AMERICA GREAT AGAIN, will have a GIANT VOICE long into the future. They will not be disrespected or treated unfairly in any way, shape or form!!!" The second, sent about an hour later, simply stated that Trump would not be attending Joe Biden's inauguration on Jan. 20.

"That same day, key Twitter staffers correctly determined that Trump's tweets did not constitute incitement of violence or violate any other Twitter policies. But pressure kept building from people like Gadde, who wanted to know whether the tweets amounted to "coded incitement to further violence." Some suggested that Trump's first tweet might have violated the company's policy on the glorification of violence. Internal discussions then took an even more bizarre turn. Members of Twitter's "scaled enforcement team" reportedly viewed Trump "as the leader of a terrorist group responsible for violence/ deaths comparable to Christchurch shooter or Hitler and on that basis and on the totality of his Tweets, he should be de-platformed."

"Later on the afternoon of Jan. 8, Twitter announced Trump's permanent suspension "due to the risk of further incitement of violence"—a nonsense phrase that corresponded to no written Twitter policy. The suspension of a sitting head of state was unprecedented. Twitter had never taken such a step, even with heads of state in Nigeria and Ethiopia who actually had incited violence. Internal deliberations unveiled by the Twitter Files show that Trump's suspension was partly justified based on the "overall context and narrative" of Trump's words and actions—as one executive put it —"over the course of the election and frankly last 4+ years."

"That is, it was not anything Trump said or did; it was that Twitter's censors wanted to blame the president for everything that happened on Jan. 6 and remove him from the platform. To do that, they were willing to shift the entire intellectual framework of content moderation from the enforcement of objective rules to the consideration of "context and narrative," thereby allowing executives to engage in what amounts to viewpoint discrimination.

"Private companies, of course, for the most part have the right to engage in viewpoint discrimination—something the government is prohibited from doing by the First Amendment. The problem is that when Twitter suspended Trump, it was operating less like a private company than like an extension of the federal government.

"Among the most shocking revelations of the Twitter Files is the extent to which federal law enforcement and intelligence agencies came to view Twitter as a tool for censorship and narrative control. In part six of the Twitter Files, Taibbi chronicles the "constant and pervasive" contact between the FBI and Twitter after January 2020, "as if [Twitter] were a subsidiary."

"In particular, the FBI and the Department of Homeland Security wanted Twitter to censor tweets and lock accounts [they] believed were engaged in "election misinformation," and [those government entities] would regularly send the company content [they] had pre-flagged for moderation, essentially dragooning Twitter into what would otherwise be illegal government censorship. Taibbi calls it a "master-canine" relationship. When requests for censorship came in from the feds, Twitter obediently complied—even when the tweets in question were clearly jokes or posted on accounts with few followers.

"Some Twitter executives were unsure what to make of this relationship. Policy Director Nick Pickles at one point asked how he should refer to the company's cooperation with federal law enforcement and intelligence agencies, suggesting it be described in terms of "partnerships." Time and again, federal agencies stressed the need for close collaboration with their "private sector partners," using the alleged interference by Russia in the 2016 election as the pretext for a massive government surveillance and censorship regime operating from inside Twitter.

"Requests for content moderation, which increasingly resembled demands, came not only from the FBI and DHS, but also from a tangled web of other federal agencies, contractors, and government-affiliated think tanks such as the Election Integrity Project at Stanford University. As Taibbi writes, the lines between government and its "partners" in this effort were "so blurred as to be meaningless."

The Deputization of Twitter

"After the 2016 election, both Twitter and Facebook faced pressure from Democrats and their media allies to root out Russian "election meddling" under the thoroughly debunked theory that a Moscow-based social media influence operation was responsible for Trump's election victory. In reality, Russia's supposed meddling amounted to a minuscule ad buy on Facebook and a handful of Twitter bots. But the truth was not acceptable to Democrats, the media, or the anti-Trump federal bureaucracy.

"In 2017, Twitter came under tremendous pressure to "keep producing material" on Russian interference, and in response it created a Russia Task Force to hunt for accounts tied to Moscow's Internet Research Agency. The task force did not find much. Out of some 2,700 accounts reviewed, only two came back as significant, and one of those was Russia Today, a state-backed news outlet.

"But in the face of bad press and threats from Democrats in Congress, Twitter executives decided to go along with the official narrative and pretend they had a Russia problem. To placate Washington and avoid costly new regulations, they pledged to "work with [members of Congress] on their desire to legislate."

"When someone in Congress leaked the list of the 2,700 accounts Twitter's task force had reviewed, the media exploded with stories suggesting that Twitter was swarming with Russian bots—and Twitter continued to go along.

"After that, as described by Taibbi, "This cycle—threatened legislation wedded to scare headlines pushed by congressional/intel sources, followed by Twitter caving to [content] moderation asks— [came to] be formalized in partnerships with federal law enforcement."

"Late in 2017, Twitter quietly adopted a new policy. In public, it would say that all content moderation took place "at [Twitter's] sole discretion." But its internal guidance would stipulate censorship of anything "identified by the U.S. intelligence community as a state-sponsored entity conducting cyber-operations."

"Thus, Twitter increasingly allowed the intelligence community, the State Department, and a dizzying array of federal and state agencies to submit content moderation requests through the FBI, which Chan suggested could function as "the belly button of the [U.S. government]." These requests would grow and intensify during the

COVID pandemic and in the run-up to the 2020 election.

"By 2020, there was a torrent of demands for censorship, sometimes with no explanation—just an Excel spreadsheet with a list of accounts to be banned. These demands poured in from FBI offices all over the country, overwhelming Twitter staff.

"Eventually, the government would pay Twitter $3.4 million in compensation. It was a pittance considering the work Twitter did at the government's behest, but the payment illustrated a stark reality: Twitter, a leading gatekeeper of the digital public square and arguably the most powerful social media platform in the world, had become a subcontractor for the U.S. intelligence community.

"The Twitter Files have revealed or confirmed three important truths about social media and the deep state.

"First, the entire concept of "content moderation" is a euphemism for censorship by social media companies that falsely claim to be neutral and unbiased. To the extent they exercise a virtual monopoly on public discourse in the digital era, we should stop thinking of them as private companies that can "do whatever they want," as libertarians are fond of saying. The companies' content moderation policies are at best a flimsy justification for banning or blocking whatever their executives do not like. At worst, they provide cover for a policy of pervasive government censorship.

"Second, Twitter was taking marching orders from a deep state security apparatus that was created to fight terrorists, not to censor or manipulate public discourse. To the extent that the deep state is using social media companies like Twitter and Facebook to subvert the First Amendment and run information psy-ops on the American public, these companies have become malevolent government actors. As a policy matter, the hands-off, laissez-faire regulatory approach we have taken to them should come to an immediate end.

"Third, the administrative state has metastasized into a destructive deep state that threatens to bring about the collapse of America's constitutional system within our lifetimes. Emblematic of the threat is the fact that the intelligence community has proven itself incapable of not interfering in American elections. The FBI in particular has directly meddled in the last two presidential elections to a degree that should call into question its continued existence.

"Indeed, the FBI's post-9/11 transformation from a law enforcement agency to a counter-terrorism and intelligence-gathering agency with seemingly limitless remit has been a disaster for civil liberties and the First Amendment. We need either to impose radical reforms or scrap it entirely and start over.

"The late great political scientist Angelo Codevilla argued that our response to 9/11 was completely wrong. Instead of erecting a sprawling security and surveillance apparatus to detect and disrupt potential terrorist plots, we should have issued an ultimatum to the regimes that were harboring al-Qaeda: You make war on these terrorists and bring them to justice or we will make war on you.

"The reason not to do what we did, Codevilla argued, is that a security and surveillance apparatus powerful and pervasive enough to do what we wanted it to do was incompatible with a free society. It might defeat the terrorists, but it would eventually be turned on the American people.

"The Twitter Files leave little doubt that Codevilla's prediction has come to pass. The question we face now is whether the American people and their elected representatives will fight back. The fate of the republic rests on the answer.[33]"

---

[33] John Daniel Davidson, "The Twitter Files Reveal the Existential Threat," *The Epoch Times*, February 15, 2023, 1. Also from *Imprimis,* Hillsdale College.

FBI PLANTING EVIDENCE

The FBI Planted Manufactured Evidence on Enrique Tarrio to Frame Him and Other Proud Boys Defendants, Defense Attorney Alleges

Not only did FBI agents and informants break into the Capitol Building and also encourage innocent people to do so, as discussed in prior chapters, they also did non-violent, nefarious, and arguably worse and more sleazy things to attack Trump supporters on or about January 6, including planting evidence as discussed below. In the FBI's Michigan 'kidnap the governor scheme,' the FBI actually admitted they planted explosives in a man's car, as discussed in the 'Michigan Kidnap the Governor' chapter.

* * *

From The Epoch Times, the planting of evidence on the Proud Boy:

"The most damning piece of evidence in the trial of five members of the Proud Boys was created by the U.S. intelligence community and planted on defendant Enrique Tarrio to frame him and others for alleged Jan. 6 crimes, an explosive defense motion alleges.

"Filed on Feb. 10 by an attorney for Proud Boys defendant Dominic Pezzola, the motion asks U.S. District Judge Timothy Kelly to declare a mistrial due to "outrageous government misconduct."

"The controversy surrounds a document titled "1776 Returns" that federal prosecutors contend is a blueprint for the Proud Boys to attack the Capitol on Jan. 6, 2021. That document was messaged to Tarrio, although defense attorneys say there is no evidence he opened, read, or forwarded it.

'Government-Created Scheme'

""It appears that the government itself is the author of the most incriminating and damning document in this case, which was mysteriously sent at government request to Proud Boy leader Enrique Tarrio immediately prior to January 6 in order to frame or implicate

Tarrio in a government-created scheme to storm buildings around the Capitol," defense attorney Roger Roots wrote in a seven-page document filed with the court.

"Charged in the case are Tarrio, Pezzola, Zachary Rehl, Ethan Nordean, and Joseph Biggs. The Proud Boys defendants are on trial in the U.S. District Court in Washington, accused of seditious conspiracy, conspiracy to obstruct official proceedings, obstruction of official proceedings, and conspiracy to prevent certain federal officers from performing their duties on January 6. Tarrio, Rehl, Nordean, and Biggs face nine criminal counts, while Pezzola is charged with 10.

"The trial is about to enter its fifth week in Kelly's courtroom.

"On Feb. 9, FBI Special Agent Peter Dubrowski testified that the "1776 Returns" document was sent to Tarrio on the messenger chat app Telegram by Erika Flores, an "erstwhile romantic interest," on or around Dec. 29, 2020.

"The PDF document describes plans to "Storm the Winter Palace," a reference to the Russian revolution in 1917. Assistant U.S. Attorney Conor Mulroe elicited testimony from Dubrowski that the document described a plan to "lay siege to Capitol Hill by strategically occupying most of the congressional office space around the Capitol," the motion stated.

"A member of the U.S. intelligence community testified before the now-defunct January 6 House Select Committee that portions of "1776 Returns" were taken from a document he authored in August or September 2020 to map out possible scenarios if there were chaos surrounding the outcome of the 2020 presidential election.

"Samuel Armes, who has done work for the U.S. State Department and the Special Operations Command, located at MacDill Air Force Base near Tampa, Florida, told the Select Committee he gave Flores a copy of his war game scenario document. He testified that he first met Flores in an online cryptocurrency group in 2017.

"Armes testified that at the University of South Florida, he had been "groomed to join the CIA and FBI." He told the Select Committee that he did not write "1776 Returns," but some of his war-game document was included in it.

Get Document to Tarrio

"According to the defense motion, Flores told the Jan. 6 Select Committee that Armes wrote the entire "1776 Returns" document and asked her to give it to Tarrio. In his appearance before the Select Committee on July 18, 2022, Armes denied authorship and asserted that Flores was "blame-shifting" and "throwing me under the bus."

""I can confidently say I've never seen this document in my life," Armes said, according to the official hearing transcript. "It uses stuff that I talked about, but even the name, I've never even heard of the name, right? So, yeah, I'm just a scapegoat, I guess, is the best way to word it."

"Armes testified that he met Tarrio in person "maybe twice" through Flores, but Tarrio was "certainly not a friend of mine."

""Was never interested in pursuing any kind of a relationship, as I was pretty familiar with what he stands for and represented, so I kept my distance," Armes told the January 6 committee.

"According to defense attorney Roots, if Flores's testimony about "1776 Returns" is true, "this means the most damning document in this trial was authored by the intelligence community—someone 'groomed' by the FBI itself. And this CIA and FBI asset requested Tarrio's friend to share the document with Tarrio just prior to January 6."

"The motion asks for an immediate evidentiary hearing on the origins and authorship of "1776 Returns," which Judge Kelly ruled in December 2022 could be admitted as evidence in the trial.

"If the information presented in the motion is deemed true by Judge Kelly, Roots wrote, the solution would be a "mistrial and dismissal of this entire case, with prejudice."

""This is either entrapment or outrageous government conduct, or both," Roots wrote. "Equally improper, it is a Brady [exculpatory evidence] violation because the Department of Justice must surely have known these revelations before putting Special Agent Dubrowski on the stand on February 9 to introduce this evidence."

"Federal prosecutors have not yet filed a response to the motion. The trial is scheduled to resume on Feb. 13. 2023.[34]

*   *   *

As an aside, the Proud Boys are a moderate, middle of the road organization, that promotes free speech, patriotism, and protecting church gatherings and free speech rallies from violent attacks from ANTIFA and violent Democrats. If the Proud Boys are extreme right-wing and violent, I have never read any evidence of that. When the idiot Biden, The Wall Street Journal, New York Post, New York Times etc label the Proud Boys as violent right-wing organization, they *never* offer any evidence or stories. These 'news' outlets and idiots, in the case of Biden, are just repeating a mantra, much like a monk repeating a chant, or a cricket endlessly vibrating its legs to make a sound, without spending money to do any investigation. In the actual news, I've only seen the Proud Boys defending churches etc, never attacking liberal rallies.

---

[34] Joseph Hanneman, "Manufactured Evidence Planted on Enrique Tarrio to Frame Him and Other Proud Boys Defendants, Defense Alleges, Court filing alleges "outrageous government misconduct" with key document" *The Epoch Times*, Feb 12, 2023.

GUILTY? LIABLE? THE JURY FINDING

EVIDENCE SUPPORTING A FINDING OF PELOSI'S CRIMINAL GUILT AND CIVIL LIABILITY

Pelosi declined Trump's several requests a few days prior to January 6 to bring in the National Guard to protect the building. She also failed to properly deploy and reinforce the Capitol Police. They report to her. She had received, prior to January 6, several intelligence reports stating that there was likely going to be violence and an attack on the building.

Pelosi lied and said she and her staff were not involved in planning for security, but emails, texts and testimony from the sergeant at arms and others proves otherwise. Thus Pelosi's credibility as a witness is tarnished as the evidence shows that she has lied.

Capitol Police under Pelosi waived Trump supporters into the building, and escorted them around the building, without kicking them out. Clearly this is entrapment. It is equivalent to a local cop planting cocaine in someone's car because the cop hates the person.

The upper tier of the FBI is strongly tied to and aligned with the Democratic party and hence Pelosi. The FBI, not Trump supporters, were the ones who attacked police, and broke into the Capitol Building.

Pelosi prohibited the January 6 Committee from subpoenaing, demanding or looking at her emails, texts and correspondence relating to January 6. Why? Is she hiding proof of her guilt? This implies that the texts and emails would prove her guilt of entrapment.

Pelosi refused to release 14,000 hours of security video taken by the security system at the Capitol Building, showing FBI informants opening the building's doors from the inside, and encouraging protesters to commit violent acts. The videos also show the police, who reported to Pelosi, inviting people into the building, and they show most protesters doing nothing more than walking around and taking photos, and they show police violently beating innocent protesters, and sending projectiles into the peaceful crowd who was congregated, legally, with a permit, outside the building. The police killed at least three protesters with beatings and projectiles. Nancy Pelosi's cop shot an unarmed, 110 pound woman, Ashli Babbitt, without any warning, when he could have easily just have handcuffed her.

Pelosi knew ahead of time that FBI informants dressed as Trump supporters would break into the Capitol Building, and so she had a film crew stationed inside the building to film the violence.

Trump had had over 100 rallies prior to January 6, and there never had been any violence. Did this change on January 6 because of FBI informants?

Why was Ray Epps never arrested after he told the FBI he told people to go into the Capitol Building, which was also captured on video tape? This implies he has some connection to the Democrat / Pelosi controlled Administrative State. Why did Adam Kinzinger of the Jan 6 Committee call Epps a hero after Epps told the committee that he told Trump supporters to "go into the building?"

* * *

Someone planted two bombs the day before the January 6 protest, one at Democrat headquarters in DC, and one at Republican headquarters. Video shows FBI informants listening on ear plugs at the beginning of the protest, outside the building, just when the Feds 'discovered' the pipe bombs outside the Dem and Repub headquarters. This caused many of the police to leave their guard of the Capitol Building, allowing FBI informants to lift the barriers so that police could then waive the protesters in toward the building. This was clearly an FBI and police frame operation.

The FBI has surveillance video of the guy who planted the bombs, but won't release it. Why hasn't he been arrested? The FBI was able to hunt down protesters simply based on the logos on their t-shirts. It appears the guy who planted the bombs worked for the FBI, and was part of the FBI frame job. Again, the evidence shows the FBI to be affiliated with the Dems / Pelosi.

The bombs were planted the night before January 6. VP Harris went to Democratic headquarters on the morning of Jan 6, before the Trump rally began. Harris's secret service escort swept the outside of the building before she went inside. The bombs were in plain view near park benches, and the secret service would have seen them. But the FBI did not want the bombs to be reported so early in the day. That would have disrupted their illegal entrapment scheme. They wanted the bombs to be reported during the Capitol Building riot, so that the police would be pulled away from the Capitol building, thus allowing FBI informants to remove barriers and entice protesters into the building. Thus, the deep state, the secret service, was involved with the illegal FBI frame job. The deep state is affiliated with the Democrats, and thus with Pelosi.

EVIDENCE IN SUPPORT OF PELOSI'S INNOCENCE

* * *

Pelosi's texts and emails, and those of her staff in the two and a half months leading up to January 6 would be direct evidence in support of her innocence or guilt. However, the January 6 committee was forbidden from looking at her texts and emails and those of her staff. Why? This prohibition is circumstantial evidence of her guilt or liability.

There is no direct evidence of her guilt or liability, unless it exists in her emails and texts.

WOULD A JURY FIND HER GUILTY OR LIABLE?

No one ever can predict what any jury will do. OJ was acquitted by a jury even though the evidence was strong against him. A jury convicted Murdaugh of South Carolina of murdering his wife and son after deliberating for only three hours, with zero direct evidence. That is, there were no eye witnesses nor video of the killings.

A lot depends on where the trial would be held. Joe Biden could rape a 17 year old intern in front of ten witnesses, and a DC juror pool, being all Democrats would find him not guilty. Garland probably wouldn't even prosecute him! A DC jury acquitted Dem Sussman despite strong evidence against him. Clearly jurors who work in the the DC, Federal administrative state have no interest in justice or fairness. If the trial was held in a red state like Florida, Texas or Alabama you would get a smarter, better informed pool of jurors who would believe in fairness and justice.

Given all the evidence, it appears likely that a reasonable jury would find Pelosi guilty in a criminal court, and liable in a civil court.

* * *

Pelosi could lose all her assets if the protesters who have been treated worse than Putin's political prisoners bring a class action law suit against her for assault, wrongful death, intentional infliction of emotional pain, abuse of power, conspiracy and RICO violations, to name just a few possible legal actions. Such lawsuits are feasible, especially given Alvin Bragg's absurd prosecution of Donald Trump for a paperwork mistake allegation involving paying Stormy Daniels. After all, with Pelosi there is gold in 'them thar hills', and an aggressive litigation attorney might want to do some digging. Maybe do some digging for gold for prosecutorial misconduct as well against the Jan 6 defendants.